THE SECRET POWER OF SPIRIT ANIMALS

THE SECRET POWER OF SPIRIT ANIMALS

Your Guide to Finding Your Spirit Animals and Unlocking the Truths of Nature

SKYE ALEXANDER

adamsmedia
AVON, MASSACHUSETTS

Published by
Adams Media, a division of F+W Media, Inc.
57 Littlefield Street, Avon, MA 02322. U.S.A.
www.adamsmedia.com

ISBN 10: 1-4405-6637-2
ISBN 13: 978-1-4405-6637-0
eISBN 10: 1-4405-6638-0
eISBN 13: 978-1-4405-6638-7

Printed in the United States of America.

10 9 8 7 6 5 4 3 2 1

Dedication

In memory of Domino, beloved friend,
familiar, and best cat ever

Contents

Introduction 9

PART I: SPIRIT ANIMALS AND HOW THEY CAN HELP YOU 11

Chapter 1: What Are Spirit Animals? 13

Chapter 2: How to Connect with Spirit Animals 23

Chapter 3: Practices and Techniques for Working with Spirit Animals 35

PART II: SPIRIT ANIMAL HELPERS 45

Animals 47

Birds 123

Insects 185

Reptiles and Amphibians 207

Fish and Sea Creatures 227

Index 259

"Animals are sacred. They are living expressions of the divine principle—the Goddess and the God manifest in living form."

—Timothy Roderick, *The Once Unknown Familiar*

Introduction

Do you feel a special kinship with a particular animal? Do you keep a birdfeeder in your yard so you can delight in watching your feathered friends? Have you always wanted to swim with dolphins or go on a whale watch? Perhaps your attraction to these creatures is more than just curiosity or amusement. Maybe you have a deeper connection with a certain animal, bird, reptile, fish, or insect—a connection that can benefit you in all sorts of ways. With a little practice, you can develop your relationships with animal helpers, discover their special powers, and gain their assistance in your everyday life.

Part I of this book introduces you to spirit animals and their long history of guiding human beings around the world. Since the beginning of time, these mysterious and wondrous creatures have played important roles in the myths and traditions of all cultures—some people even consider them to be divine. You'll also learn practices and techniques that will let you gain access to the secrets shamans around the globe have known for millennia.

In Part II you'll meet 201 spirit helpers, from the tiny ant to the giant whale—even some mythological creatures—who are eager to befriend you. You'll learn how to recognize them when they appear, and how to call upon them when you need their help. You'll also learn to decipher the messages they bring to you, for these spirit beings serve as guides and teachers—they can even foretell the future.

Each entry in Part II describes characteristics you are likely to possess if a particular animal, bird, reptile, fish, or insect is your totem—undoubtedly, you'll recognize traits and behaviors you share with your spirit guide. You'll also find out how to work with your primary spirit creature and when best to use a particular animal's powers. And you'll discover how to interpret these beings as signs and omens.

As you become more familiar with these magical and mystical creatures, you'll develop the ability to journey into the supernatural world where they reside. You'll also expand your understanding of the natural world in which you live. So come along now, with an open mind and an open heart, listening not only with your ears but with your whole being. Behold what these amazing animals are waiting to share with you.

Part I

Spirit Animals and How They Can Help You

Chapter 1

What Are Spirit Animals?

In ancient times, people in many parts of the world believed spirit animals lived in an invisible realm that intersects with our own physical one. These spirit beings helped our ancestors in countless ways, from providing protection to offering healing wisdom to predicting the future. Early humans considered these animal guides and guardians as types of deities—somewhat like angels—and paid homage to them. Anthropologists believe the famous paintings on the Trois Frères cave walls in Montesquieu-Avantès, France, which date back some 15,000 years, may have been put there by Paleolithic peoples to petition the aid of animal deities in the hunt, or to thank them for providing food and shelter.

You've probably heard of "totems." The term refers to an animal, bird, reptile, fish, or insect with which you feel a strong and perhaps inexplicable affinity. A totem is your primary spirit animal guardian, or the guardian of your family or group. Some indigenous tribes in North America carved totem poles depicting the various animals that protected their people and brought blessings to them. Archeologists have discovered animal figurines buried in tombs around the world, perhaps placed there to guide human souls into the spirit realm.

Different people hold varying ideas about exactly what spirit animals are. Some traditions say that animal guides once lived on earth as physical creatures, and passed over into the spirit world after death. Your beloved Fluffy may have taken off her cat suit, but she's still nearby in spirit. Other views suggest that spirit beings never actually existed in the flesh—although their earthly counterparts may embody the spirits' energies. Still others tell us that spirit animals can assume the forms of physical creatures when they want to and can move between the worlds of ordinary and nonordinary reality at will. A deer that darts across your path and then disappears might be a "real" deer, but then again . . .

People who study and work with spirit animals generally agree on one thing, however: These entities willingly offer us their help, and they do so whether or not we realize it. If you learn to recognize their presence in your life and understand their unique abilities, you can tap their special powers and use them to intentionally enhance your own well-being.

One Animal Helper or Many?

How many spirit animals can you call upon for help? Most researchers and authorities believe you have at least one totem that serves as your guardian, teacher, and guide. Your personal totem may invite other animals to assist on occasions when you need a little extra help or when you're facing a challenge that requires the special characteristics of another creature. Let's say, for instance, your primary spirit animal is the bull and you usually charge ahead into situations with great force. But now a circumstance needs some finesse. Your bull totem might invite a fox to serve as a temporary guide, helping you cleverly maneuver through the intricacies of the matter.

Some sources say you have a single, primary animal guardian throughout your life, although other beings may show up from time to time as needed or to bring you messages. In Siberia, indigenous people believe that each member of a tribe has his or her own reindeer guardian. Other metaphysical researchers think that you have several spirit animals that direct different facets of your life. In your initial forays into the realm of spirit animals, invite your primary animal guide to make itself known to you and try to sense its presence. After you've established a rapport with this entity, you might attempt to connect with other creatures too.

Celtic and Old European clans believed that certain animal deities oversaw entire groups of people. Irish clans called their members griffins, wolves, deer, etc., and individuals took their names from these animals. MacCon, for example, means "hound's son." Animal guardians performed numerous functions for a clan, including protecting its warriors in battle. The legends of King Arthur tell of Owein's band of ravens fighting against Arthur. Sometimes men wore animal skins or affixed horns to their helmets to solicit help from their totems during combat. Others carried flags depicting these creatures, or painted images on their bodies to bring them success. Many family crests or coats of arms include animals, and those animal symbols convey distinct meanings. A bear, for instance, represents protection; a lion equates with courage; a dog signifies loyalty. The crest of the Rothschild family—one of the most powerful families in the world—features a lion, a phoenix, and a unicorn.

We see a version of this expressed today by our athletic teams. The Denver Broncos, the Boston Bruins, the Miami Dolphins, the St. Louis Cardinals, and the Chicago Bulls are just a few of the dozens of animal-named teams found among the professional leagues. Wouldn't you rather have a magnificent animal as your team's mascot instead of a pair of red socks or a net?

Is Your Zodiac Animal Your Totem?

Both Western and Chinese astrology link zodiac signs with animals. Zodiac means "circle of animals." You probably know your sign—but is the creature connected with it your totem? Maybe, though not necessarily. Regardless, you'll surely share some traits with your zodiac animal. If you're a Capricorn with the goat as your symbol, you persevere one step at a time and can climb to great heights. If you're a Leo, you may have regal bearing like the lion and proudly assume your role as a leader. Whether or not your zodiac animal is your totem, you can ask it to lend you its special powers when you need its assistance.

Animal Deities from Around the World

Throughout time, in cultures around the world, deities have taken the forms of animals, birds, reptiles, and even insects. The ancient Egyptians' pantheon included lots of gods and goddesses who appeared as animals, birds, or hybrid creatures, among them the cat goddess Bast, a jackal-headed god named Anubis, the falcon-headed Horus, and Sekmet, the lion-headed goddess. The Chinese recognize four gods of heaven and earth: the dragon, phoenix, tiger, and tortoise. Quetzalcoatl, or "the Feathered Serpent," was one of the Aztecs' most important gods. Ganesh, the elephant deity who helps humans overcome obstacles, is a popular figure among the Hindu gods and goddesses. The Aboriginal Australians worship a deity known as the Rainbow Serpent, and in Japan the god Ryūjin is depicted as a dragon, whose servants include fish and sea turtles. Among the indigenous peoples of North America, many animal spirits show up—often as trickster figures, such as the Coyote—and deities frequently shapeshift from spirits to animals or birds.

White Buffalo Calf Woman

The Lakota, Dakota, and Nakota tribes revere a deity known as the White Buffalo Calf Woman who they say taught the people how to live harmoniously with each other and with all of nature—including the animals, or "four-leggeds." She taught the native people ceremonies, songs, and dances and gave them holy objects. Before leaving, she transformed herself into a white buffalo calf, an animal still held sacred among the Plains Indians as a sign of change. White buffalo are extremely rare, and when a white calf was born in 1994 the native people considered it an omen that predicted a time transition.

Some gods and goddesses don't actually assume animal bodies, but they interact with special creatures. The Norse god Odin (Woden), for instance, keeps two ravens—Munin (memory) and Hugin (thought)—as companions. Foxes serve as symbols and messengers for the Japanese deity Inari. In the Christmas story, Jesus's birth was attended by animals in a stable. Buddhism connects eight protector deities with the twelve creatures in the Chinese zodiac. Western astrology, too, links gods and goddesses with the zodiac animals, among them Venus with the bull, Mars with the ram, Jupiter with the centaur, and Neptune with fish.

Scratch the surface of virtually any culture's mythology and you'll find deities sporting fur, feathers, scales, or fins, sometimes in awesome combinations. It seems people everywhere, since prehistoric times, have found the world's myriad creatures infinitely fascinating and worthy of respect.

Animal Powers and Their Elemental Connections

You're probably familiar with the four elements—earth, air, fire, and water—especially if you've studied astrology, the tarot, or other metaphysical subjects. It's easy to see the manifestations of these elements in the physical world. But each element also corresponds to specific modes of expression, energy patterns, and realms of experience.

- **Earth:** sensation, practicality, material resources
- **Air:** mental activity, intellect, communication
- **Fire:** inspiration, spirit, action, motivation
- **Water:** emotions, intuition, creativity

Spirit creatures can be grouped into these four elemental categories, too. Understanding the meanings of the elements will help you to comprehend the significance of spirit beings and use their unique powers to your advantage. To determine which element a spirit creature belongs to, notice where it spends most of its time. Most mammals are terrestrial, meaning they live on land; that connects them with the earth element. Most birds fly through the sky, so their element is air. Fish and shellfish reside in water, hence they correspond to the element of water. Reptiles often move between land and water, so they relate to both the earth and water elements. Insects, too, reside in various places, and thus have connections with different elements.

Some physical creatures occupy more than one type of habitat. For example, a duck can fly, swim, or waddle about on land. Therefore, this animal embodies the qualities of air, water, and earth. To interpret the meaning of the physical duck's spirit counterpart, examine the qualities associated with all three elements. This will enable you to make the most of this spirit bird's powers. Animals such as monkeys don't fly, but their habitat high in the treetops and their penchant for swinging from tree to tree gives them a link to the element of air as well as earth. Some insects, such as moths and butterflies, change their forms and environments during their lifespans. If the butterfly is your totem, pay attention to its life cycles—and your own. In your youth, you might resonate with its grub/earth qualities, but as an adult you may shift your modus operandi and focus on airy activities. The better you understand a spirit creature's nature, the more adept you'll become at working with it.

Mythical Composite Creatures

Folklore and mythology tell tales about all sorts of half-breed creatures who combine the forms of more than one species. Mermaids, for example, merge the bodies of humans and fish. The centaur mixes a human torso with a horse's back and legs. Many Egyptian deities feature bird or animal heads atop human bodies. The Sphinx does the reverse: it has a human head and a lion's body, and sometimes a giant bird's wings. These magical beings blend the best of both worlds, and they can be amazingly powerful spirit guides if you choose to work with them. It's a good idea to read the legends surrounding them, however, before you start hanging out with them.

The Significance of Seasonal and Diurnal Cycles

Some creatures tend to be more active at certain times of the day or year. Others change locales seasonally. Bears, for instance, hibernate during the winter. Bats spend the day resting in their caves and fly out to feed at night. When the weather turns cold, many birds migrate from the northern regions to more salubrious southern climes. And some sea creatures, such as the salmon, travel long distances back to their homes to spawn.

Paying attention to the rhythms of various animals can give you insight into their powers, and your own. Are you a sun worshipper who heads to the tropics during the cold months? Or do you prefer to curl up in your cozy den? Are you an early bird who catches the worm, or a nighthawk who enjoys staying up into the wee hours? These traits can provide clues to discovering which animal is your totem.

If you decide to work with a spirit being other than your totem, it's important to notice the animal's cycles. For example, you'd be better off asking an owl to accompany you on a long nighttime drive instead of a dove.

Chapter 2

How to Connect with Spirit Animals

How will you know your spirit animal when you meet it? As we said earlier, you have at least one primary spirit guide—an animal, bird, reptile, fish, or insect—and other temporary or secondary beings that show up on an as-needed basis. Your main spirit creature has been with you since infancy, perhaps even before you were born. Over time, it has probably appeared to you in numerous ways, both physically and in dreams or visions, even though you might not have realized it at the time.

Have you always felt a powerful attraction to a particular animal, even one that seems a bit unusual, such as a porcupine or an ostrich? As a child, did you have a special stuffed creature that you adored more than all your other toys? If so, that might represent your spirit guardian. Have you felt an incredible link with a pet that goes way beyond normal affection? Perhaps your spirit animal connected with you through that beloved pet. Maybe you even look like an animal, with the long golden mane of a lion or the hooked nose of a hawk.

But just because you find an animal attractive or intriguing doesn't mean it's your spirit guide. Sometimes spirit animals show up to teach you what you need to know or to assist you in certain situations—and they might not be ones you'd choose.

That's a good point to remember when you try to contact your spirit animal. You don't choose your spirit guardian—it chooses you. It also solicits the aid of other creatures when you need specific powers it doesn't possess.

Is Your Pet Your Totem Animal?

Some traditions believe only animals in the wild can serve as totems, although not everyone shares this idea. Others say domesticated animals link us to their wild relatives. A black cat, for example, might be a smaller, tamer version of a black panther. But just because you are fond of your cat, dog, or horse doesn't mean it is the embodiment of your primary spirit guide. Do you feel a profound connection with a pet that transcends ordinary affection? Can you communicate intuitively with it? Do you sense it has a special purpose or reason for being in your life? If so, your pet could be your totem's earthly counterpart.

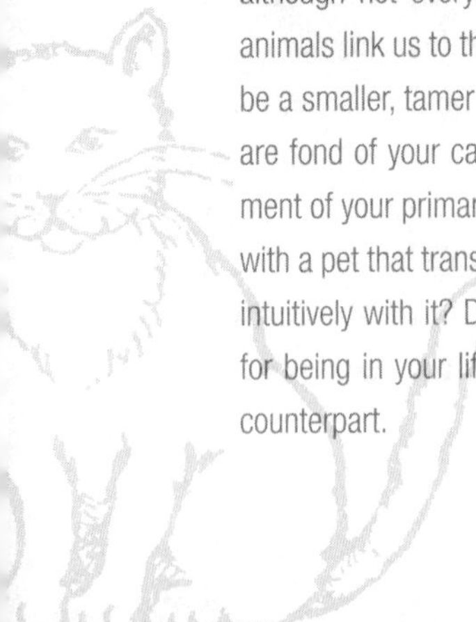

Meeting Your Primary Spirit Animal

Are you ready to meet your spirit animal guide? The first step is to ask it to make itself known to you. Your purpose for getting to know your primary spirit animal is to establish a strong bond between you, one that will last a lifetime.

Find a quiet, comfortable place where you won't be disturbed, and sit or lie down. Be still. If you know how to meditate, use this technique to calm your mind and slip gently into a light trance state. Otherwise, just relax. Breathe slowly and deeply, and attempt to keep your thoughts from wandering.

Try not to hold any expectations about what spirit being will appear. You might be fond of a particular animal or want a beautiful, dynamic, or exotic creature to be your guide, but that one might not be your totem. If you're looking for a lion to show up and roar, you may be surprised or disappointed if your spirit guardian turns out to be a mouse. Remember, no being is better than any other. The one that comes to you does so for a good reason, and it has many wondrous blessings to bestow on you. Show it respect, and it will share its wisdom and unique powers with you. It will be your constant companion, loyal friend, and devoted helper.

Your totem animal might reveal itself to you right away and you'll instantly identify with it. Perhaps you'll see a vision of it in your mind's eye or sense its presence near you. But that doesn't always happen. It could take a few days or longer before you recognize your guide. Perhaps the animal will show up in a dream, or you may encounter its physical counterpart in nature. It can choose countless ways to make your acquaintance. Again, try not to hold expectations about how or when your spirit guide will appear—just trust that it will when the time is right and that the experience will be a positive one.

If your initial attempt doesn't produce the results you desire, don't despair. Once you've made your intention known, it's only a matter of time before you meet your spirit animal. While you're waiting, you might want to "prime the pump," so to speak. Watch animal shows on TV. Look at magazines that picture animals, such as *National Geographic*. Spend time in nature observing wildlife. Pretty soon, your animal helper will realize that you are sincere and come forward.

Tips for Meeting Your Totem

Keep these suggestions in mind as you attempt to connect with your animal guide:

- Be sincere and respectful—believe your spirit helper will appear.
- Be patient—it might take a while before you can identify with your totem.
- Keep an open mind—the creature that appears to you might not be what you expect.
- Pay attention—your spirit animal might turn up suddenly or in a way you hadn't anticipated.

Recognizing Spirit Animals When They Show Up

Spirit animals come into your life to help you. Your primary guide is always there, ready to assist you in any situation. It freely offers guidance, protection, insight, healing, and many other gifts. You can also request favors from other spirit beings in special instances—or your totem animal will solicit their assistance. Often these beings lend their powers to you for a short period of time, for a particular purpose. An elephant, for example, can help you overcome an obstacle; an eagle can let you see things from a new perspective; a butterfly can guide you through a change in your life.

Sometimes you'll see an animal in nature, and if it's a creature you wouldn't ordinarily find in your locale, this could be a poignant sign for you. You might spot a picture of your animal helper on a TV show, a magazine, or a billboard beside a highway. If your animal guide is a buffalo and you find an old buffalo nickel on the sidewalk, take notice; your spirit animal has something to share with you.

Notice your reaction when something like this happens. Many people experience an "aha!" moment. Others may feel a chill or tingling sensation, an inexplicable fascination with the animal, or a flash of recognition.

Animals often appear when they want to bring you a message—they may even speak to you through symbols. Let's say you're driving along the road and a Dodge Ram truck cuts right in front of you, forcing you to sit up and pay attention. The incident could be a spirit ram's way of contacting you.

Instead of getting mad, think about what a ram signifies. Power? Daring? Aggression? Competitiveness? Is it telling you to tackle a matter head on? To engage an adversary forcefully and directly? Are you being too aggressive or not aggressive enough? In Western astrology, the ram is the symbol of Aries, the first sign of the zodiac. Therefore, a ram's appearance might presage the beginning of something new. In Part II, we'll examine the symbolic meanings of different animals, birds, reptiles, fish, and insects—but what's most important is what the creature means to you.

Spirit Animals in Dreams

Spirit animals frequently show up in dreams. When your rational, analytical waking mind is at rest, your subconscious can communicate with you. If you've ever studied dreams or psychology, you know the subconscious speaks in symbols. Animals are some of the most common dream symbols. That's partly because spirit beings can get through to you more easily while you're sleeping; you're less skeptical and more receptive. Animals also possess so many distinctive characteristics that they can quickly and effectively convey information to you. If you see a cheetah, for instance, you immediately associate it with speed. If you dream of an owl, you automatically link it with wisdom.

When spirit animals appear to you in waking life, they bring messages intended to guide you. The same is true of dream animals. Sometimes they even give you a glimpse of the future.

In the book of Genesis, an Egyptian pharaoh dreamed about seven fat cattle followed by seven lean cattle, and the lean ones gobbled up the fat ones. A young Hebrew man named Joseph interpreted the dream as a warning that Egypt would experience seven years of fruitfulness and bounty, followed by seven years of famine. As a result of the dream, the pharaoh managed to prepare Egypt and store up plenty of food to carry the people through the lean times.

When a creature turns up in your dream, notice not only its obvious traits but also what actions it performs. Does it behave in a normal way or act in an uncharacteristic manner? Also pay attention to how you react and interact with the animal. Do you befriend it? Run away from it? These observations can provide clues to its purpose for contacting you. If a particular creature appears regularly in your dreams, it could be your totem visiting you—or it might be a spirit animal who's trying really hard to get your attention.

Interpreting the Meanings of Colors

In addition to enriching our lives visually, colors impact us psychologically and physically. As a result, we attach special symbolism to colors. When a creature shows up in your waking life or in a dream, pay attention to its color; that can help you to interpret its significance. Goldfish, for instance, represent abundance. Crows are linked with mystery and magic. Different cultures assign different meanings to colors, but the ones listed here are generally accepted in the West.

- **Red:** Passion, vitality, aggression
- **Orange:** Expansion, enthusiasm, confidence
- **Yellow:** Optimism, creativity, happiness
- **Green:** Growth, prosperity, health
- **Blue:** Tranquility, insight, peace
- **Indigo:** Security, trust, permanence
- **Purple:** Wisdom, spirituality, leadership/power
- **Pink:** Joy, affection, friendship
- **White:** Purity, protection, innocence
- **Black:** Mystery, magic, inner wisdom, the unconscious
- **Brown:** Practicality, stability
- **Gold:** Wealth, good luck, masculine power
- **Silver:** Good fortune, intuition, feminine power

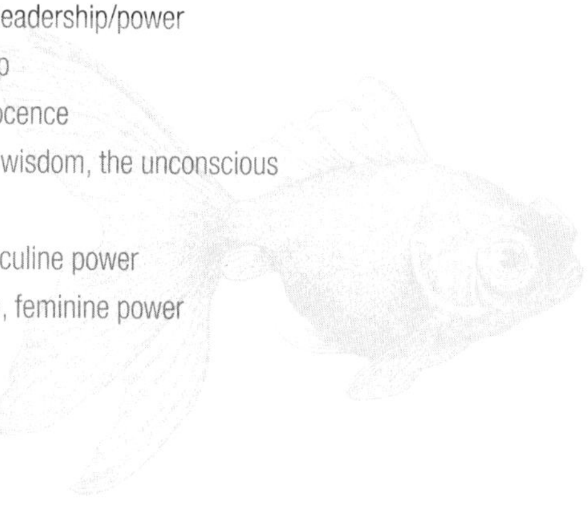

What Are Spirit Animals Trying to Tell You?

Learning to interpret an animal's meaning can be tricky at first. With a little study and practice, however, you'll become adept at figuring out what spirit animals are trying to tell you. Like any skill, animal communication gets easier the more you do it. When an animal appears to you in a dream, vision, or in the physical world, ask yourself these questions to determine its meaning.

First, consider the animal's most obvious traits.

- What is its species?
- What are its most notable physical characteristics?
- What color is it?
- How does it move?
- What sounds does it make?
- What unique qualities or abilities do you associate with it?

Second, examine the creature's habitat and behavior.

- Where does it live?
- How does it cope with its environment?
- What does it eat?
- How does it interact with other creatures?
- How does it breed and care for its young?
- What does it like/dislike?
- Is it more active during certain seasons or times of the day/night than others?

Third, pay attention to what the animal is doing when you see it and how you react to it.

- Is it behaving normally or doing something unexpected?
- Is it alone or with other creatures?
- Is it in its usual habitat or someplace you'd never expect to see it?
- How do you feel about the animal? Are you delighted? Afraid? Curious? Perplexed?

You probably won't need to consider all these factors—sometimes you'll understand the animal's meaning right away. For example, if you're hurrying down a sidewalk in Manhattan and see a turtle, it could be a signal that you need to slow down. As a rule of thumb, the more unusual a situation and/or the more powerful your feelings, the more important the animal's message is.

Animal Terminology

Think about how you use animal terms in connection with other things, as well as various alternative meanings an animal's name might have. For example, an attractive person might be called foxy and a homely one a dog. You might refer to someone who betrays you or reveals a secret as a rat. You "duck" to avoid injury or an attack. "Bear" means to endure, and "bat" means to hit. In dreams, especially, a creature's appearance might be a play on words or symbolize something other than the obvious.

Symbiotic Relationships Between Animals

You might also find it useful to examine the creatures with which an animal normally interacts. Symbiotic relationships can provide additional information about your totem animal or other temporary spirit animal helpers—and about yourself. When you see an animal in nature or in a dream, think about the other beings that play roles in its life.

If your animal is a predator, what is its prey? Foxes, cats, and some birds eat small rodents. Wolves hunt deer and, in packs, can bring down larger species such as elk or moose, but their diet also includes plenty of small rodents. Lions feed on gazelles, antelope, and zebras. Robins gobble up worms. Flamingos like shrimp. Conversely, if your totem is on another animal's menu, what creatures threaten it?

Strange Companions

Not all symbiotic animal relationships fall into the predator-prey category. Some creatures get together for surprising mutual benefits. Egrets and oxpeckers, for example, ride on the backs of large mammals including elephants, water buffalo, and hippos, and eat parasites that collect on the beasts' bodies. Some birds even crawl into crocodiles' mouths and clean their teeth by feasting on food particles trapped there.

The creature(s) associated with your totem can reveal a side of you that you might not be aware of. In Carl Jung's terminology, it could signify your "shadow side"—the subconscious part that usually lies hidden or unacknowledged. If you want to learn more about your primary spirit guide—and yourself—study its relationships with other beings.

The explanations in Part II provide a good beginning for interpreting the significance of animals in nature, dreams, and visions. You may want to investigate further and learn more, especially when working with your primary animal guide. You'll find lots of information in other books and online that can take you deeper into the world of spirit guardians.

Chapter 3

Practices and Techniques for Working with Spirit Animals

Now that you've determined which animal is your totem, you're ready to deepen your relationship with it. Spirit animals want to help you and they can, in myriad ways. That's a good reason for learning to work with them. But spirit creatures can also show you how to become more loving and accepting of yourself and others. They can teach you how to respect your true nature, to express your innate talents, and to be the best that you can be.

It takes time to develop a relationship with your spirit animal, just as it takes time to build a friendship with a human being. You're establishing a bond based on mutual trust, so be patient. Set aside a period of time every day to communicate with your totem. Observe the animal's behavior and appreciate its uniqueness. Try to see things from its perspective. Enjoy the growing affection between you. In this chapter you'll learn techniques to help you create a profound connection with your totem animal that will last a lifetime.

Honoring Your Totem Animal

Showing respect and admiration for your totem animal is an essential part of working with it. This creature has a great deal to offer you, so of course you'll want to express gratitude for its gifts. You can do this in a variety of ways.

- Find pictures of your totem in magazines or online and display them in your home or workplace.
- Learn as much as you can about it.
- Draw, paint, or sculpt images of your totem.
- Write a poem or story about your spirit animal.
- Watch animal shows on TV.
- Wear jewelry or clothing with the animal's picture on it.
- Get a tattoo of your animal.
- Go to a park, beach, farm, wildlife sanctuary, zoo, or other place to see your totem in the flesh.
- Join an animal welfare organization.
- Give money to a charity that protects animals and/or their habitat.

- Buy only cruelty-free products.
- Become a vegetarian.

You might want to set up an altar in your home and dedicate it to your totem. Here you can place images, figurines, etc., of your spirit guide and make offerings to it. If your totem is a hummingbird, for example, you could put a vase of red flowers on your altar. Use your imagination and come up with creative ways to show appreciation for your spirit animal's assistance.

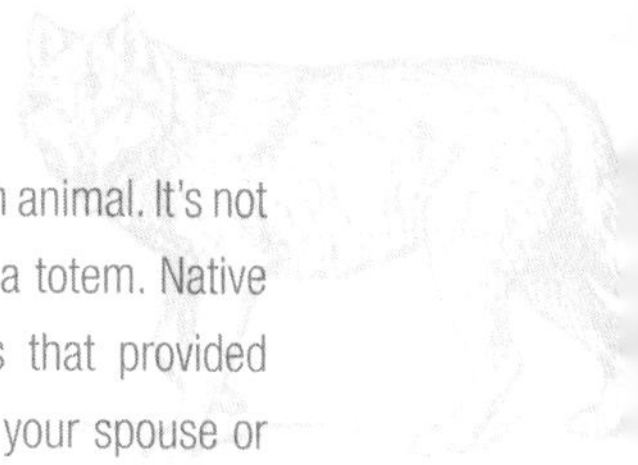

Sharing a Totem with Someone Close

You and someone you love might have the same totem animal. It's not surprising to find people in the same family sharing a totem. Native American tribes were allied with particular totems that provided guidance and protection to the entire tribe. You and your spouse or partner may have the same totem, especially if you share many characteristics, interests, and behaviors. Or, your totems may come from the same animal family. For example, if one of you is more friendly and domestic, that person's totem might be the dog, whereas the more assertive or daring person could have a wolf totem.

Animal Medicine

Native Americans use the term "medicine" when working with spirit animals and nature. They don't mean medicine like aspirin or antibiotics, however. In this sense, medicine refers to an animal's power and magic, as well as its ability to heal us at every level. According to Dr. Loretta Standley, tribal member of the Eastern Band Cherokee Indians, "Animal medicine refers to the healing aspects that a particular animal brings to our consciousness.

This would mean anything that supports, strengthens, restores, empowers, or revives the spiritual body, as well as the physical body."

An animal offers you its medicine to help with something you need at a particular time. Your totem isn't the only animal that can give you medicine—all creatures can, and in fact, many do throughout your lifetime. The medicine you receive may change from day to day. One day you might need hawk medicine in order to see more clearly; another day squirrel medicine could help you prepare for the future.

When you spot an animal in nature or a dream, it may have come to bring you its medicine. Animals also appear to us through television, magazines, books, or even conversations. If you feel suddenly or strongly drawn to a particular animal, bird, etc., it could be a signal that you need that creature's medicine right now. Consider the animal's distinctive characteristics to understand what message it brings. Is a lion telling you to roar? Is a badger showing you how to dig deeper to discover the truth? In Part II, you'll learn how to use the medicine of 200 different creatures to reap benefits in every area of your life.

Familiars, Totems, and Pets

The term "familiar" refers to a special animal, bird, or other creature that works with a person to produce magical results. Remember Harry Potter's owl? A familiar's physical and spiritual qualities can help bring healing, protection, prosperity, and many other blessings. Sometimes a beloved pet might be a familiar, but that's not always the case. Your totem might share its powers through a familiar, but your totem doesn't necessarily serve as your familiar, nor is your familiar necessarily your totem. All creatures, however, can teach you valuable lessons, including how to be more loving.

Act Like an Animal

You've heard the saying imitation is the highest form of flattery. To strengthen your connection with your totem or another spirit animal, try imitating it. If you want to communicate with a dove or a meadowlark, try whistling its song. Play a woodpecker's tapping sound on a drum.

Emulate your totem's movements. Trot like a horse; hop like a kangaroo; creep stealthily like a panther. Hold your arms out like a cormorant drying its wings. Pretend you're a bee and smell flowers. If your totem is a crane, heron, or flamingo, try standing on one leg the way it does.

A number of yoga poses (asanas) are named for animals because they resemble the creatures' postures. In Cobra, for example, you lie on your stomach and push your head and shoulders upward, like the snake lifting its head to look around. In Pigeon, you tuck one leg under you and stretch the other out behind, while straightening your torso and puffing out your chest like a pigeon does. Assuming an animal asana can give you a physical sense of how it might feel to be that creature.

Native Americans dance to solicit an animal's medicine. They might even dress in garments made with the feathers or skins of the creatures. You can, too. You don't necessarily have to enact an authentic tribal dance—just move in a manner similar to that of the animal. If you choose to wear a leather jacket, snakeskin belt, or alligator shoes, remember to honor the creature whose sacrifice has enabled you to partake of its power.

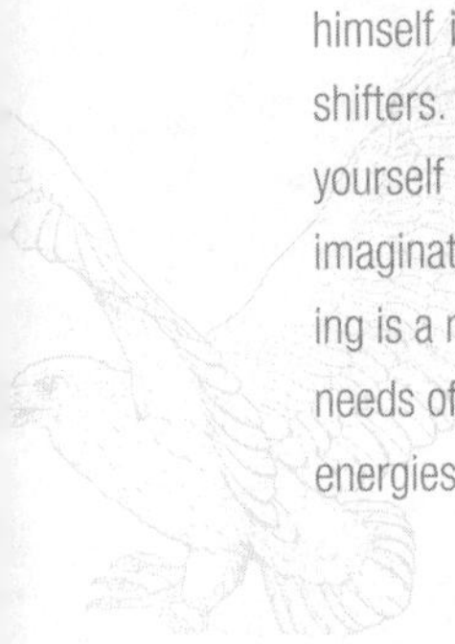

Shapeshifting

The myths of many cultures describe the act of "shapeshifting," by which one species changes into another. In one version of the Arthurian legends, the great magician Merlin teaches Arthur to turn himself into a hawk. Native American stories also speak of shapeshifters. Shapeshifting, however, doesn't mean actually transforming yourself into an animal—you assume the animal's characteristics in imagination. As Ted Andrews explains in *Animal-Speak*, "Shapeshifting is a matter of controlling and shifting your own energies to fit the needs of the moment—being able to draw upon those qualities and energies necessary."

Shamanic Journeying

Shamans, magicians, medicine men and women, visionaries, and mystics believe the material world parallels a nonphysical one. Some philosophies say that the earth emerged from a spiritual dimension that holds the templates for everything we witness on our planet. You can travel with your totem animal into nonphysical or nonordinary realms of existence. This type of journeying is also a good way to meet other spirit animals and learn from them.

What Is a Shaman?

Shamans can be found in many cultures, including those of the Celts and Native Americans. These men and women understand both the natural world and the spirit realm and can move easily between these dimensions. They can also shapeshift into animals if they don't want someone to recognize them. Usually shamans enter a nonphysical world in imagination, in order to access wisdom that will benefit themselves and/or others. They may use music, drumming, dancing, or other techniques to alter their awareness to a trancelike state that allows them to perceive beyond the physical level. The process of traveling between the worlds is sometimes called journeying.

Do you want to journey into other dimensions? You can. If you've already established a comfortable relationship with your totem animal, ask it to lead the way. Don't worry that you'll get lost or that something scary might happen to you in this other world. Your spirit animal guardian will be there to guide, protect, and teach you.

Find a place where you won't be disturbed. Turn off the TV, phone, and any other distractions. You might want to light a candle, burn incense, play relaxing instrumental music, or hold a quartz crystal to help you shift your awareness. If you have a particular reason for wanting to journey—to gain information or insight into a specific problem, for instance—hold that purpose in your mind as you begin. When you're ready, close your eyes and breathe slowly, deeply.

1. In your mind's eye, see a place in nature that you consider beautiful, serene, and safe. It could be someplace you've been before, or a spot that exists only in your imagination.

2. Sense or see your spirit animal nearby. Notice it beckoning to you.
3. Your spirit guide leads you to an opening, such as a hole at the bottom of a tree, a cave, a tunnel in the ground, or a whirlpool in a body of water. As you watch, the animal slips easily into the opening. Follow it.
4. See or sense yourself moving through the opening and coming out in another place. It may or may not resemble anyplace you've ever seen before. Whatever you experience is okay.
5. Explore this area with your totem animal at your side. Observe what's around you, using all your senses. Listen to what your spirit guide says and pay attention to what it shows you.
6. Perhaps you'll notice other creatures in this place. What are they? Does one or more of them approach you with a message? Let your intuition receive this information.
7. Spend as much time in this place as you wish. When you feel ready to return to your ordinary reality, thank the animals you've met here for helping you.
8. Retrace your steps, back to the passageway through which you entered the spirit realm. Follow your animal guide into the opening again and return.
9. When you're ready, open your eyes and emerge gently into your everyday world once more. Thank your spirit animal guide for its assistance.

It's a good idea to write down what you experienced right away, so you don't forget it. Whatever happened is important. You might even want to keep a journal of your journeys. Even if you don't understand what you perceived while in the spirit world, note it—at a later date, it might make sense to you.

Vision Quests

A vision quest, like a shamanic journey, takes you into another realm of existence to gain knowledge and insight. A traditional vision quest involves physically going out into nature alone for a period of time, in order to communicate with the inhabitants of the nonordinary world. During a vision quest you might realize your life purpose, gain insights that can promote healing, reach a better understanding of yourself, overcome your fears, or experience some other type of wisdom teaching. Often people meet spirit animals as well as other spirit teachers while on vision quests.

Making Animal Charms and Fetishes

You can partake of an animal's power by carrying a charm or fetish that honors the animal. These objects possess magical energies that can provide protection, healing, and other things you desire. Sometimes charms contain feathers, bits of fur, bone, teeth, claws, or other animal ingredients—no, we're not talking about eye of newt and toe of frog. Nor should you ever harm an animal in any way for the purpose of creating a lucky charm. To invoke an animal's blessings, only use what the animal has shed naturally.

Let's say, for example, you choose to work with deer medicine to help you become more graceful, gentle, or fleet of foot. You could add a small piece of deer antler to a charm or "medicine bag." Want to be happier? Create a charm that includes a bluebird's feather. You don't need actual animal parts to make an effective charm; you can use images of an animal. Cut out pictures from a magazine, download an online image, or draw the animal yourself. Or you can purchase a small figurine or piece of jewelry that represents the animal.

When you're ready to create your magic charm, find a place where you won't be disturbed. Silence the TV, phone, and other distractions. Light a stick of incense or a bundle of sage and waft the smoke around the area where you'll be working in order to psychically cleanse the area—be careful not to set anything else on fire! Briefly hold the objects you'll put in your charm in the smoke to cleanse them, too.

You might also want to include crystals, dried herbs, or other ingredients in your charm. Place all the items you've collected into a small silk or cotton pouch and tie it closed with ribbon or string. Wear it or carry it in your pocket to attract the animal's power and enhance your own. (For more information about making talismans, amulets, and fetishes, see my book *The Everything® Spells & Charms Book, 2nd Edition.*)

Part II

Spirit Animal Helpers

"When we learn to speak with the animals, to listen with animal ears and to see through animal eyes, we experience the phenomena, the power, and the potential of human existence, and it is then that the animals are no longer our subordinates."

—Ted Andrews, Animal-Speak

ANIMALS

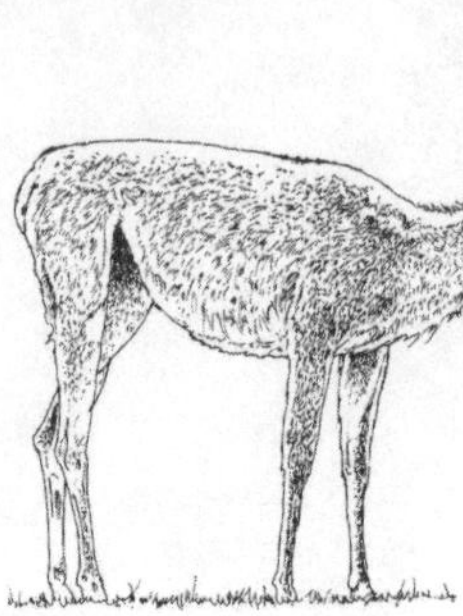

Alpaca

Characteristics: Like its relative the llama, the alpaca is native to the Andes Mountains in South America. If this is your animal guide, you may like being in high places, and perhaps enjoy mountain climbing. You might also seek spiritual heights and devote yourself to gaining ancient wisdom. Your endurance enables you to thrive even in harsh conditions. Alpacas have long been prized for their precious fur, and people with this totem often have abundant, lustrous hair. In addition to your beauty, your gentle disposition and friendly nature attract people to you, and you probably have many friends and acquaintances. Generous to those you love, you willingly share your gifts to enrich the lives of others.

Strengths: Beauty, hardiness, friendliness, generosity

Weaknesses: Vanity

How to use this animal's power: Call upon an alpaca to help you enhance your natural beauty or to make the best of your physical qualities. This animal can also teach you how to get along with people and live peacefully within a community. If you are beginning a spiritual quest, ask an alpaca to accompany you.

Symbolic meanings: When you see an alpaca while awake or dreaming, it may advise you to be more gentle or sociable. It might also encourage you to be generous with your time, money, or abilities. Sometimes this animal's appearance means you'll soon receive a gift.

Anteater

Characteristics: Naturally curious, you tend to poke your nose into other people's business and situations that intrigue you, which could serve you well in a career as a reporter, researcher, or investigator. Health and healing might also interest you, especially nutrition. You aren't satisfied with the obvious; rather, you probe beneath the surface to discover the truth. Once you undertake something, you "dig in" and proceed with determination and thoroughness, rooting around until you get what you want. The independent type, you usually rely on your own skills and methods instead of following the crowd.

Strengths: Determination, curiosity, independence

Weaknesses: Nosiness, finicky eating habits, food sensitivities

How to use this animal's power: If you want to find something you've lost, an anteater can help you poke around until you locate it. Ask an anteater to help you dig into a project and give it your all. An anteater can also teach you better eating habits and help you stick to your diet.

Symbolic meanings: If you encounter an anteater in waking life or in a dream, it might advise you to poke deeper into a matter to discover what's going on behind the scenes. An anteater's appearance could also mean either you're being too nosy or that someone else is sticking his nose into your business. Sometimes an anteater shows up when you need to pay more attention to your diet.

Antelope

Characteristics: The antelope's incredible speed is one of its most distinctive traits—it can run up to sixty miles per hour and leap high in the air, so that it almost seems to fly. If this is your totem animal, you probably display great speed, agility, and grace either physically, mentally, or both. Your ability to sense danger is also highly developed, enabling you to pick up on people or situations that might be detrimental to you so you can get out of the way in time. Antelopes can survive in inhospitable climates, including deserts, and like them you may be quite hardy or resilient.

Strengths: Speed, agility, grace, intuition, resiliency

Weaknesses: Defensiveness, flightiness

How to use this animal's power: Do you play a sport in which speed is important? Ask an antelope to lend you its amazing ability to outdistance opponents. An antelope can also teach you how to endure hardships, leap over obstacles, or make the best of difficult situations.

Symbolic meanings: The presence of an antelope in real life or a dream could alert you to possible danger or warn you to pay attention to what's going on around you. It might also urge you to speed up, either to accomplish a task on time or to avoid problems.

Armadillo

Characteristics: Like this small, armored animal, you are very good at protecting yourself and your loved ones. However, you don't like to reveal your true self and can be overly skeptical or defensive. You want to understand things at a deep level and eagerly delve beneath the surface to discover what lies at the heart of a matter. A natural detective, you like to explore unknown areas and might be interested in psychology or occult subjects. You're also good at figuring out what makes other people tick, and probably have a well-developed intuition. This can cause you to feel empathy and compassion for others.

Strengths: Protectiveness, persistence, intuitiveness

Weaknesses: Defensiveness, secretiveness, destructiveness

How to use this animal's power: When you feel threatened and need to protect yourself or others, call upon an armadillo to assist you. If something doesn't seem quite right and you want to know what's really going on, an armadillo can help you unearth the truth.

Symbolic meanings: If you see an armadillo while awake or dreaming, it might be a warning that you need to hone your defenses. An armadillo may also appear to tell you to dig deeper into a situation, rather than accepting what's obvious. It could advise you to look deeper into yourself and your motivations, perhaps even to consider undergoing therapy.

Badger

Characteristics: Known for your fearlessness, you never back down from a fight and can be a fierce adversary. Because the badger has very strong jaws, you may use your verbal powers as well as your physical ones to best your enemies. Independent and self-reliant, you're not particularly sociable and probably don't feel close to many people, even your family members. Like your totem animal, you eagerly dig beneath the surface to uncover what lies below. This inquisitiveness can lead you to seek ancient or occult wisdom and to probe secrets and mysteries of all kinds.

Strengths: Courage, independence, self-reliance, communication skills

Weaknesses: Aggressiveness, antisocial behavior, insensitivity

How to use this animal's power: When you feel threatened, call upon a badger to lend you its courage. Ask this animal to strengthen your communication skills when you need to counter an opponent verbally or get your point across firmly. A badger can also help you discover something that's been hidden from you.

Symbolic meanings: If you see a badger while awake or dream about one, it might advise you to dig deeper into a matter—what's obvious may not be the truth. A badger's appearance can also tell you to be more independent and self-reliant or to stand up for yourself. Don't let others fight your battles for you.

Bat

Characteristics: Bats are known for their ability to find their way around in the dark, so if this is your totem you likely possess keen intuition that enables you to see what other people don't. Your "sonar" helps you maneuver through life with ease and skill, allowing you to avoid some problems and soar above others. Perhaps you also have a highly developed sense of hearing and can discern the true meanings behind what people say. Many people fear bats and erroneously consider them evil or dangerous. With this spirit animal as your guide, you can courageously face your fears and deal with changes constructively.

Strengths: Intuition, flexibility, fearlessness

Weaknesses: Obliviousness, phobias, oversensitivity

How to use this animal's power: Are you hiding something from yourself? A bat can help you face up to what you fear, especially fear of change or death. Because the bat is the only mammal that flies, it can raise your awareness and give you a different perspective. Call upon a bat to guide you through life changes or challenging situations.

Symbolic meanings: If you see a bat in the waking world or a dream, it can advise you to face your fears and not close your eyes to what's happening. It might tell you to listen more carefully, too. A bat's appearance may also presage an upcoming change.

Black/Brown Bear

Characteristics: You possess tremendous strength and can be fierce, but you're usually gentle and even rather shy . . . unless someone provokes you. You're probably quicker and more agile than you appear, and people tend to underestimate your capabilities. Extremely protective of your loved ones, you will go to great lengths to keep them safe. Although you have a playful side, you need to withdraw from society for periods of time to be alone and rest.

Strengths: Strength, speed, protectiveness, loyalty, peacefulness

Weaknesses: Reclusiveness, poor judgment

How to use this animal's power: When you need extra strength, physically or emotionally, ask a bear to lend you its power—especially if you're facing a threat of some kind. Are you having trouble handling a problem or making a decision? Let a bear guide you to discover your own inner wisdom.

Symbolic meanings: Encountering a bear in the waking world or in a dream can indicate that you need to withdraw from activity for a while to rest, or, conversely, that you should come out of your cave and be more sociable. Perhaps you need more sleep to keep up your strength. A situation may arise soon that requires you to use your power to protect yourself or others.

Beaver

Characteristics: Hard working and industrious, you like to stay busy and usually have several projects going on at any time. You enjoy building things and seeing the results of your labor. Once you start something, you see it through to completion. Pragmatic and security-conscious, you're willing to put in long hours to acquire money, a nice home, and material goods. Your determination and resourcefulness enable you to succeed at whatever you do.

Strengths: Perseverance, practicality, creativity, industriousness

Weaknesses: Stubbornness, materialism

How to use this animal's power: Do you have a project to finish in a short period of time? Ask a beaver to help you work steadily and stay on track. If your job requires you to put in extra effort, let a beaver come to your aid. Beaver power can also enhance your creativity and productivity.

Symbolic meanings: Seeing a beaver while awake or in a dream can mean you are working too hard or, conversely, that you need to work harder to reach your goal. It can also advise you to be more practical and use your resources in a more constructive manner.

Black Panther

Characteristics: The panther shares many traits with the leopard and jaguar, but its black coloring aligns it with the mysteries of the night and feminine power. Like your totem, you display exceptional beauty, grace, and strength, and people find you fascinating. However, you're the independent type and usually prefer to go it alone. You use your keen senses and intuition to accomplish your goals, intently "stalking" your objective with precision and cunning. You know the value of keeping silent so as not to waste energy or reveal too much about yourself. Instead, you watch and listen closely to others, waiting for them to expose themselves and give you an opportunity to pounce. In mythology, the black panther is associated with magic as well as the secrets of life, death, and rebirth.

Strengths: Beauty, grace, strength, skill, feminine power, intuition, independence

Weaknesses: Secretiveness, ruthlessness, unsociability

How to use this animal's power: If you need to accomplish a goal secretly, ask a black panther to guide you. This animal can teach you how to hone all six senses and use them more effectively. Invite a panther to help you connect with feminine power and hidden wisdom.

Symbolic meanings: The presence of a black panther in real life or a dream could advise you to be silent and not reveal your intentions. Its appearance might alert you to a coming opportunity—get ready to pounce. This animal also symbolizes awakening to your powers or passions.

Boar, Wild

Characteristics: You charge at life with gusto and courage, and go after what you want without hesitation or fear. A risk taker with a wild streak, you play by your own rules, not society's. Nothing much daunts you and you enjoy challenges. Your competitiveness, physical strength, and vitality could make you a good athlete. Your aggressiveness, however, can put other people on the defensive, and you may make enemies without realizing it. Confrontational and quick-tempered, you can be inconsiderate or combative at times and might need to learn to control your anger.

Strengths: Physical power, courage, enthusiasm, directness

Weaknesses: Aggressiveness, destructiveness, impatience, contrariness, quick temper

How to use this animal's power: A wild boar can help you overcome your fears and face up to challenges. If you've been avoiding something or someone, invite a boar to join you in confronting it boldly. Ask a boar to lend you its sharp tusks to defend yourself or cut through obstacles.

Symbolic meanings: If you see a wild boar in the waking world or a dream, it may tell you to confront someone or something directly: don't be afraid to take a stand. It might also advise you not to behave in a boorish manner.

Bobcat

Characteristics: Like this small wild cat, you tend to be a loner and prefer a quiet, secluded life to one filled with people and activity. You understand the importance of being still and looking within for guidance. Perhaps you're a creative individual who needs lots of solitary time to do your art, writing, etc. However, you can tend to hide away in order to avoid dealing with others or facing life's challenges. Sensitive and intuitive, you use your sharp powers of observation to protect yourself and to accomplish your objectives. You may even possess psychic ability and, like the bobcat, feel most alive at night.

Strengths: Independence, intuitiveness, keen observation skills

Weaknesses: Secretiveness, unsociability

How to use this animal's power: The bobcat can help you learn to be still and quiet instead of wasting energy in excessive busyness. If other people are draining your energy, this animal can show you how to be independent and lead a more solitary life. It can also help you keep a secret.

Symbolic meanings: If you see a bobcat in the real world or dream of one, it might tell you to stop socializing so much and spend more time alone. Conversely, it could mean that you're cutting yourself off from people and need to be more sociable. This spirit animal may also urge you to look within for answers.

Buffalo/Bison

Characteristics: Like your totem animal, you may be quite big and strong. But even if you aren't large physically, you possess inner power, endurance, and fortitude. When obstacles come your way, you push through them with determination. However, you prefer to take the path of least resistance whenever possible and not waste your time or energy. As a result, you can achieve a lot and usually get what you want, especially when it comes to material success. Usually you manage your resources well, too, although some of you tend to be hoarders.

Strengths: Physical power, forthrightness, resourcefulness, material success

Weaknesses: Unpredictability, insensitivity, possessiveness

How to use this animal's power: Want to make more money? The buffalo can show you how to use your abilities more successfully. If you must overcome problems or obstacles, ask a buffalo to lend you its strength. This animal can also show you how to take it easy and stop struggling—you don't have to force your way through life.

Symbolic meanings: The appearance of a buffalo in the waking world or a dream can be a sign that wealth or abundance is coming to you. It can also advise you not to waste your resources. Sometimes a buffalo recommends that you become more spiritual and less materialistic.

Bull

Characteristics: If the bull is your totem animal, you may be very powerful, especially physically. However, you also possess inner fortitude. Most of the time you prefer to take it slow and easy, though you can move quickly when you need to, and at times you charge into situations impulsively. The bull has long symbolized fertility; therefore, you probably have a strong sex drive and enjoy all sorts of sensual pleasures. You might also possess creativity or a fertile mind. Astrology links the bull with the zodiac sign Taurus, an earthy, physical sign, and people with this spirit animal totem tend to be practical, grounded, and materialistic.

Strengths: Physical power, fertility, productivity, determination, sexual stamina

Weaknesses: Stubbornness, insensitivity, combativeness, pushiness

How to use this animal's power: Want to improve your sex life? Ask a bull to lend you its sensuality and fertility. A bull can help you be creative in other ways as well. If you're too flighty or idealistic, this spirit animal can teach you how to be more practical and bring your ideas down to earth.

Symbolic meanings: When a bull shows up in waking life or in a dream, it often symbolizes sexual power. Perhaps you're not expressing your sexuality fully, or, conversely, you're being too promiscuous. A bull's appearance may suggest you're overly attached to your possessions and the material world. It can also urge you to charge ahead instead of hanging back.

Camel

Characteristics: Like your totem animal, you possess amazing survival skills and can get along in even the most harsh or barren circumstances. Your power lies in knowing how to conserve your resources and use them effectively. You also know how to pace yourself, so you don't waste energy or time on things that won't benefit you. As a result, you often succeed where others fail. Hardy and resilient, you capably handle challenges—physical, emotional, financial, and spiritual—that might daunt other people, without getting stressed out or anxious. Therefore, you could enjoy a long and healthy life.

Strengths: Endurance, self-sufficiency, survival skills, efficiency

Weaknesses: Stubbornness, selfishness, materialism

How to use this animal's power: Call upon a camel when you need to be more practical and efficient; it can help you manage your financial, physical, and psychic resources wisely. This animal guide can also teach you how to become more self-sufficient and to find whatever you need within yourself.

Symbolic meanings: If you see a camel in the waking or dream world, it might advise you to use your resources more carefully and effectively. The camel's message is "waste not, want not." Its appearance could also predict a time of lacking or hardship ahead and warn you to store up what you'll need for the future.

Cat

Characteristics: Your agility, grace, and cleverness enable you to adapt to changing circumstances, and even in difficult situations you usually land on your feet. Infinitely curious, you get bored easily and are always ready for a new adventure. Your playful nature attracts many companions; however, you're basically a loner and prize your independence. Sleep and comfort rank high on your list of priorities. Looks are important to you, too, and you probably spend a lot of time grooming. You like to bask in the sunshine, but probably do your best work at night.

Strengths: Grace, beauty, dexterity, perceptiveness, dignity, intelligence, self-reliance

Weaknesses: Restlessness, indolence, antisocial behavior, vanity, finickiness

How to use this animal's power: If you've been working too hard or shouldering many responsibilities, a cat can show you how to have fun and take it easy. The cat can also help you find ways around problems or get out of scrapes. Because cats can see in the dark, this is a good animal to call on when you want to see something more clearly.

Symbolic meanings: Seeing or dreaming of a cat can mean you need to play or relax more. It might also alert you to a possible challenge that will test your ingenuity. Perhaps you need to be more independent and self-sufficient, or to engage your curiosity and explore beyond your comfort zone.

Cheetah

Characteristics: You're known for your speed, whether on the playing field or in the business world, and you easily outpace your competitors. Once you set a goal for yourself, you pursue it in high gear. Not easily intimidated, you bring your strength, skill, and stealth to bear in all endeavors. Your independent nature and killer instinct make you a powerful force with which to be reckoned, and you usually get your way. However, if you don't achieve your aims quickly, you might lose interest.

Strengths: Speed, focus, vitality, independence, intelligence, courage

Weaknesses: Impatience, aggressiveness, lack of consideration for others

How to use this animal's power: When you need to think or act quickly, call upon a cheetah to lend you its speed. A cheetah can also help you overcome adversaries, defend yourself, or meet challenges head on.

Symbolic meanings: Seeing a cheetah while awake or dreaming can mean you need to act fast or pick up your pace in some area. It may also suggest that you're being too aggressive or ruthless, and not taking other people into account. On the other hand, a cheetah might show up to urge you to be more assertive.

Chimpanzee

Characteristics: Your playful spirit and friendly personality delight other people, and you probably have many companions who enjoy being around you. You know how to have a good time and don't let the world's troubles get you down. However, you can be temperamental, and if annoyed you may react with hostility. Toward family and friends you display affection and devotion, nurturing all who seek out your loving care. Your curiosity leads you to explore many subjects and to experience as much as you can in life. Known for your intelligence, you learn quickly and readily share your knowledge with others. Challenges intrigue you, and you use your resourcefulness and imagination to solve problems creatively.

Strengths: Intelligence, playfulness, sociability, curiosity

Weaknesses: Talkativeness, laziness, unpredictability

How to use this animal's power: A chimpanzee can show you how to have a good time and be more playful. If faced with a problem or puzzle, ask a chimp to help you solve it.

Symbolic meanings: If you encounter a chimpanzee in waking life or in a dream, it may mean you need to lighten up and play more. Its appearance might also suggest you need to be nurtured, or that you seek the love and companionship of friends and family.

Chipmunk

Characteristics: Always busy, you have many interests and rarely waste time in nonproductive activities. You don't waste your resources, either, and have a knack for making wise investments. You're concerned with accumulating wealth, material goods, property, and other things you believe will bring you security, so that once you've achieved your aims you can take time to rest. However, you can become too attached to your possessions and equate your self-worth with your material worth.

Strengths: Determination, pragmatism, efficiency, agility, sociability

Weaknesses: Indecisiveness, hoarding, possessiveness, greed

How to use this animal's power: Call upon chipmunk power when you need to be more productive or to use your abilities more effectively. A chipmunk can also show you how to get the things you want in life, and to increase your holdings.

Symbolic meanings: If you see a chipmunk while awake or dreaming, it may be advising you to stop wasting time and get busy making money. Conversely, it could mean that you're too attached to material possessions and investing too much energy in acquiring wealth, to the detriment of other areas of your life.

Cougar/Mountain Lion

Characteristics: Speed, stealth, and strength are among your many notable qualities and these powers enable you to succeed in life. Once you make up your mind to do something, you act decisively and forcefully. When an opportunity arises, you quickly jump on it. You're willing to take risks and learn from your mistakes, therefore each experience makes you wiser and stronger. Your assertiveness, however, can irritate cautious or conservative types who may try to hold you back.

Strengths: Speed, stealth, assertiveness, decisiveness

Weaknesses: Aggressiveness, ruthlessness, misuse of power

How to use this animal's power: When a challenge or threatening situation arises, call upon a cougar to provide the courage and strength you need. If you're letting others call the shots, ask a cougar to show you how to take charge of your own life. This animal can also help you be more decisive.

Symbolic meanings: If a cougar appears to you, whether you're awake or dreaming, it may be telling you to assert yourself. It might also advise you to use your power in a constructive rather than destructive way. Sometimes this animal's appearance can warn that a situation is coming in which your abilities will be tested. An opportunity might arise soon—get ready to grab it.

Cow

Characteristics: Unlike people with the bull as a totem, you're known for your gentle disposition and patience. Instead of charging ahead rashly, you go about the business of living in a slow, calm, and methodical way and don't waste energy on unimportant things. You have a strong domestic streak; home and family are central to your happiness. You love children and express your nurturing nature with all who need you, young and old alike. You might even choose a career that uses this quality, such as nursing or teaching. The ancient Egyptians depicted the nurturing goddess Hathor as a cow, and people with this totem feel a deep connection to feminine power.

Strengths: Compassion, patience, gentleness, nurturing nature

Weaknesses: Laziness, complacency

How to use this animal's power: A cow can show you how to care for yourself and other people, especially children and family members. It can also teach you patience and perseverance, and how to slow down to enjoy life.

Symbolic meanings: If you see a cow in either the physical world or a dream, it might advise you to slow down, take it easy, and don't waste energy. This animal's appearance could mean you need to nurture yourself or others. It may also recommend connecting with your feminine side, whether you're male or female.

Coyote

Characteristics: In mythology, the coyote often appears as a trickster figure. If this is your totem, you may enjoy playing tricks on people, or might present yourself in a way that fools others—you aren't always what you seem. You have a playful, fun-loving side and like games of all kinds. You're also very sociable; your friends and family are important to you. Clever and wily, you don't like to struggle to get what you want and can usually find an easy way around difficulties. Many of you possess well-developed communication skills that enable you to share your ideas creatively and convincingly.

Strengths: Cleverness, adaptability, playfulness, communication skills

Weaknesses: Laziness, deceitfulness

How to use this animal's power: If you find yourself in a tricky situation, call on a coyote to lead you out of the difficulty. If you've been working too hard or feel discouraged, ask a coyote to show you how to have more fun. This animal can also help you verbalize your ideas effectively.

Symbolic meanings: When you spot a coyote while awake or in a dream, it may warn you to be more crafty and clever. A problematic situation may arise soon that will require you to be wily or flexible. Someone may be playing a trick on you. A coyote's appearance can also encourage you to have fun—life isn't meant to be a struggle.

Deer

Characteristics: Gentle and peace loving, you seek a quiet, simple life in the company of congenial people, and maintain close ties to your family. The hectic pace, stress, and competition of the business world can seem intimidating to you. You tend to be timid, nervous, and sensitive, and often run away from challenges rather than facing them squarely. Although you possess grace and beauty, you prefer to fade into the background rather than stand out from the crowd.

Strengths: Grace, beauty, sensitivity, gentleness, swiftness, humility

Weaknesses: Nervousness, inconsistency, timidity

How to use this animal's power: If you find yourself in a situation that requires grace and sensitivity, a deer can show you how to behave. A deer can also help you retreat from stressful situations and find serenity. Use deer power when you need to be alert to possible danger.

Symbolic meanings: Seeing a deer in the waking world or in a dream can mean you're being too sensitive about something; conversely, you may need to use more compassion, tact, and delicacy. Perhaps you should draw less attention to yourself or be more modest. A deer might also encourage you to distance yourself from a problematic person or conflict.

Dog

Characteristics: Your loyalty is legendary, and no matter what happens you stick by your loved ones. Good-natured and affectionate, you like companionship and probably have lots of friends with whom you enjoy good times. Your easygoing manner, playfulness, and willingness to see the good in everyone draw people to you. When a friend needs help, you're always right there. However, you may lack good judgment and can let others take advantage of you.

Strengths: Loyalty, protectiveness, cheerfulness, keen powers of observation

Weaknesses: Lack of discrimination, laziness, dependency on others

How to use this animal's power: Do you want to attract friends? Ask a dog to help you expand your circle of companions. If you feel unhappy or discouraged, a dog can show you how to enjoy life and have more fun. Dog power can also help you "sniff out" people and situations, so you can discern the truth.

Symbolic meanings: Seeing or dreaming about a dog can mean you need more affection or companionship. Or, it can advise you to be more loving and less critical of yourself or others. A dog's appearance might also warn you to protect yourself or someone you care about: if something doesn't "smell right," pay attention.

Dolphin

Characteristics: Dolphins are known for their great intelligence, and if the dolphin is your totem animal you, too, possess superior cognitive ability. You learn quickly and enjoy sharing information with others. Like the dolphin, who plunges hundreds of feet into the sea, you delve deeply into areas that interest you. Your keen intuition also gives you insight into things other people don't understand. Friendly and good-natured, you probably have a large circle of companions and you're always ready to play. However, you may lack discrimination and might hang out with people who aren't good for you.

Strengths: Intelligence, sociability, communication skills, intuitiveness, grace

Weaknesses: Talkativeness, laziness, gullibility

How to use this animal's power: When you want to attract friends or make a positive impression on people, let a dolphin show you how to be more likeable. Need some extra brainpower to solve a challenging problem or learn a new skill? A dolphin can give you the boost you seek.

Symbolic meanings: If you see a dolphin in real life or meet one in a dream, it might advise you to be more playful and sociable—have fun! A dolphin could recommend using your intuition as well as your intelligence to get to the bottom of a matter.

Donkey

Characteristics: You possess great strength and tenacity—inner as well as outer—and can handle burdens that might overwhelm other people. You usually shoulder the responsibilities placed upon you without complaint and patiently persevere with whatever task you're required to perform. You don't like to be rushed, however, and once you've chosen a course you can be inflexible. If pushed, you may respond loudly and angrily. You may have a strong protective streak and watch out for those who aren't as hardy or strong as you. When danger approaches, you fight back with surprising force and can be a formidable adversary.

Strengths: Endurance, persistence, patience, physical strength, protectiveness

Weaknesses: Stubbornness, noisiness

How to use this animal's power: When you must bear a challenging responsibility or heavy burden, ask a donkey to lend you its strength. This animal can also help you to be patient when dealing with difficult problems and people who annoy you.

Symbolic meanings: If you see a donkey in the physical world or in a dream, perhaps you need to stop being so stubborn. Maybe this animal is advising you to shoulder more responsibility or to use your strength to assist others. In some cases, a donkey appears to warn you to be on the alert for danger.

Elephant

Characteristics: Your great strength—both outer and inner—is one of your most obvious qualities, but even if you aren't large you're quite powerful. Difficulties that might thwart other people don't daunt you, and you persist until you accomplish your goals. You have brains as well as brawn, and your memory is amazing. With friends and loved ones, you're very affectionate, and you probably have a circle of companions who mean a lot to you. Your familial relationships, too, tend to be close and warm, and you're extremely loyal to the people you care about. But if someone crosses you or hurts your feelings, you can hold a grudge for a long time.

Strengths: Outer and inner strength, intelligence, sociability, loyalty

Weaknesses: Emotional sensitivity, vengefulness, stubbornness

How to use this animal's power: When a problem arises that you feel is too big for you to handle alone, call upon an elephant to help you push past the obstacle. Ask an elephant to lend its power whenever you need extra strength to accomplish a physical or mental task.

Symbolic meanings: When an elephant appears to you, it could advise you to use your strength to overcome an obstacle—don't give up. It might also encourage you to help others who aren't as strong as you. If you've been focusing too much on physical things, an elephant may tell you to pay more attention to intellectual concerns.

Elk

Characteristics: Like the elk, you possess great strength and stamina, and can marshal your power to achieve long-term goals, both physically and mentally. Your persistence and ability to hang in there when the going gets tough enable you to go the distance. As a result, you may succeed when other less hardy people give up. Although you enjoy socializing with others, you tend to hang out with people of your own gender rather than interacting regularly with those of the opposite sex. A homebody, traveling doesn't interest you much. Instead, you prefer to stick with what's familiar, and can be very protective of your home and family.

Strengths: Physical strength, stamina, endurance

Weaknesses: Awkwardness around the opposite sex, narrowness

How to use this animal's power: When you need extra stamina, ask an elk to lend you its strength. If you've grown impatient because things aren't moving ahead as quickly as you'd like, an elk can teach you how to dig in and persevere over the long haul.

Symbolic meanings: If you spot an elk in the waking world or a dream, it might urge you not to give up—to push harder and pursue your goal with more tenacity. This animal may also show up when you're spending too much time hanging out with your buddies; it advises you to expand beyond your immediate circle for companionship.

Ferret

Characteristics: The ferret shares some traits with its relative the weasel, including keen observation skills. Intelligent and intuitive, you quickly size up people and conditions. Your ingenuity enables you to slip in and out of situations unnoticed, and to maneuver around obstacles. Known for your uncanny ability to "ferret out" secrets and information, you tunnel deep beneath the surface to dig out hidden truths and essential knowledge. With your innate "hunting" skills, you could succeed as a detective or researcher. But you're much more affectionate, friendly, and playful than people with the weasel totem, and enjoy companionship.

Strengths: Intelligence, intuition, cunning, stealth, ability to focus, sociability

Weaknesses: Slyness, sneakiness

How to use this animal's power: When you need to get to the bottom of a tricky matter or discover what's going on behind the scenes, ask a ferret to show you what lies hidden from view. A ferret can also guide you through difficulties and help you find a way out of an unpleasant situation.

Symbolic meanings: If you see a ferret in the physical world or a dream, it might advise you to dig deeply and get to the bottom of something. It might also suggest that you need to use cunning or intuition to resolve a matter. If you've been working too hard, a ferret may show up to tell you it's time to play.

Fox

Characteristics: Known for your cleverness and cunning, you have an uncanny knack for getting out of scrapes and coming out on top in difficult situations. Your quick wit and agile mind enable you to solve problems that baffle others. Your keen intuition also allows you to instantly size up people and circumstances, usually to your advantage. Charming, graceful, and imaginative, you have no trouble attracting people of both sexes. However, you sometimes use your charm or beauty to manipulate others—you might even trick people to get what you want.

Strengths: Ingenuity, intuitiveness, grace, beauty

Weaknesses: Dishonesty, superficiality

How to use this animal's power: If you find yourself in a tricky situation that requires cunning or skill, ask a fox to come to your aid. A fox can also help you learn a new subject, ace an exam, or make an impressive presentation. Want to win someone's affection? The fox can show you how to charm and delight that person.

Symbolic meanings: When you see a fox while awake or dreaming, it may warn you to be alert—someone or something may not be what it seems. Use your powers of observation as well as your intellect and intuition. A fox might also tell you to be wilier.

Giraffe

Characteristics: Like the giraffe, you might be quite tall, but regardless of your physical height you can see things other people miss. Your broad perspective on life enables you to avoid some of the problems others face, and not allow little things to bother you. As a result, you tend to be congenial and optimistic much of the time. If the giraffe is your totem, you're probably both intuitive and intelligent. The world of ideas fascinates you. However, you might "have your head in the clouds" and ignore practical matters.

Strengths: Intuition, perception, friendliness

Weaknesses: Impracticality, naiveté

How to use this animal's power: When you need to see the big picture or want another perspective on a matter, ask a giraffe to assist you. A giraffe can also help you to shift your focus—quit worrying about little annoyances and enjoy life more.

Symbolic meanings: When you see a giraffe in waking life or a dream, it could be telling you to stop dwelling on petty details and look at the whole in order to appreciate what's really important. A giraffe's appearance might also suggest that it's time to stop being an airhead and come down to earth.

Goat

Characteristics: You readily go where other people can't or won't. With your fearless nature, strength, and determination, you can scale the heights and achieve a great deal. You don't let obstacles stand in your way and persist until you accomplish your goals, no matter how lofty. Cautious and practical, you believe in taking things one step at a time rather than rushing blindly into situations. You rely on your own abilities and experience instead of depending on other people. At times you can be stubborn, though, and refuse to try something new or listen to the wisdom of others. Goats are also associated with sensuality and materialism, and if this animal is your totem, you can tend to overindulge in physical pleasures.

Strengths: Perseverance, pragmatism, self-reliance, hardiness

Weaknesses: Stubbornness, hedonism

How to use this animal's power: If you're having trouble staying focused on a task, ask a goat to teach you determination, patience, or perseverance. A goat can also show you how to become more self-reliant and successful.

Symbolic meanings: An encounter with a goat, either in waking life or a dream, may mean you need to be more ambitious or try harder to accomplish a goal. Conversely, it could indicate that you're working too much and need to play more. A goat might also advise you either to express your sexuality more fully, or rein it in and be more discriminating.

Gopher

Characteristics: You're not satisfied with superficialities; you want to understand the deeper meaning of life and to uncover hidden wisdom. Your search for purpose and fulfillment could lead you to join a group of like-minded individuals with a common goal, for you can accomplish more if you ally yourself with others. Friendly and cooperative, you are probably an active force in your community, and may have an extensive social network. You strive to create something of lasting value, and could succeed in the construction or landscaping business. Be careful not to take on more than you can handle, though, and dig yourself into a hole.

Strengths: Sociability, cooperation, creativity

Weaknesses: Destructiveness, lack of discernment

How to use this animal's power: A gopher can teach you how to dig more deeply into a situation, in order to discover what lies beneath the surface. It can also help you dig into yourself to discover your hidden talents and find your true path in life.

Symbolic meanings: If you see a gopher in the here and now or a dream, it might advise you to be more ambitious or industrious—are you acting as a "go-for" instead of expressing your talents fully? A gopher may appear when you need to dig more deeply to find your purpose.

Gorilla

Characteristics: Like your totem, you command attention and respect. Your intelligence and strength make you a natural leader. Self-confident, decisive, and resourceful, you believe you can accomplish anything you set out to do, and you usually succeed. You function best when your life has order and structure—you'll even step in and try to organize other people's lives, whether they want you to or not. Gorillas live in groups known as troops, and people with this totem often fit well into military careers. Whether you are guarding your country or your family, you marshal your forces and fiercely protect what you consider yours.

Strengths: Intelligence, self-confidence, leadership ability, loyalty, physical strength

Weaknesses: Materialism, aggressiveness, dominating or bullying behavior

How to use this animal's power: When you need to take charge of a situation and assume a leadership role, ask a gorilla to lend you its power. A gorilla can also show you how to get your life in order, and to handle responsibilities with determination.

Symbolic meanings: If you see a gorilla while awake or dreaming, it might tell you to take command of a situation. It could also mean that you're being too domineering and need to let others do things their own way. A gorilla's appearance can encourage you to devote more time to your family.

Griffin

Characteristics: This mystical creature combines an eagle's head and wings with a lion's body, and represents the merger of intellectual and physical power. Like your totem, you have a regal presence and inspire awe in all who meet you. You possess nature leadership ability, but instead of seeking worldly success you aim for a higher purpose, and can guide your followers to spiritual enlightenment. In mythology, the griffin guarded hidden treasures, and you might serve as a guardian of occult secrets and inner riches.

Strengths: Leadership ability, vigilance, balance of body, mind, and spirit

Weaknesses: Inner conflict, arrogance, spiritual hubris

How to use this creature's power: A griffin can show you how to discover the treasure that lies within, and how to use it advantageously. It can also teach you how to transcend material concerns and reach for lofty goals.

Symbolic meanings: If you see a griffin in a dream or elsewhere, it advises you to balance mind, body, and spirit. If you've become enmeshed in material considerations, a griffin could suggest turning your attention to spiritual things—seek for gold within, not in the external world. A griffin's appearance might also warn you to guard your secrets or something you treasure.

Groundhog

Characteristics: The groundhog is considered a harbinger of spring, and you may be the person who alerts others to forthcoming changes and opportunities. You're able to see things on the horizon before they materialize because you have a highly developed sense of intuition. Just as the groundhog burrows into the earth to hibernate for long periods of time, you need to withdraw for periods of time for rest and renewal. You delve deeply into yourself and into the hidden world to learn the secrets of life, death, and beyond. You use your resources wisely and like to see the results of your efforts. Patient and persistent, you work diligently to achieve your goals and stick with a task even if it takes a long time.

Strengths: Psychic ability, vision, determination, inner wisdom

Weaknesses: Inability to set healthy boundaries, tendency to withdraw from everyday life

How to use this animal's power: When you need help seeing what lies ahead, ask a groundhog to share its secrets with you. This spirit animal can also guide you on inner journeys of self-discovery and help you connect with your own inner wisdom. If you're embarking on a long-term project, invite this animal to join you. When you need to find out what's going on beneath the surface, ask a groundhog to help you find answers.

Symbolic meanings: If you see a groundhog while awake or dreaming, it might advise you to stop hiding away in your burrow and come out into the world. Perhaps you're becoming too introspective, and avoiding contact with other people. This animal can also suggest that you should dig beneath the surface to discover what lies within. A groundhog's appearance could signal the beginning of something new, or awakening into a new phase in life. Perhaps it is advising you to build for the future and work harder to accomplish your goals; conversely, it may suggest that you need to take a break and rest.

Horse

Characteristics: You have a restless nature and need a lot of freedom; you don't want anyone to fence you in. Independent, you champ at the bit when you feel restricted, and insist on doing things your way. You love to travel and probably like sports, especially running and horseback riding. Your charisma draws admirers to you; people find you sexually attractive and enjoy your beauty, confidence, and sense of adventure.

Strengths: Speed, strength, grace, vitality, athletic ability, beauty, sexual prowess

Weaknesses: Restlessness, rebelliousness, inconsistency

How to use this animal's power: Invite a horse to assist you in a challenge that requires speed, strength, or extra vitality. If you feel corralled or burdened, a horse can help you jump over obstacles and guide you to new experiences and adventures.

Symbolic meanings: Seeing or dreaming about a horse suggests you seek more independence and excitement. You could be going on a trip or beginning a new life journey. Perhaps you long to shake off the load you're carrying and run free for a while. You might also wish to express your sexuality more fully or freely. To better interpret its meaning, notice whether you're having fun riding the horse, or if you're hanging onto a stampeding steed for dear life.

Hyena

Characteristics: Unconventional and eclectic, you march to a different drummer. You have your own code of ethics and don't follow society's dictates. You're not antisocial, however; you work well with others, and understand the value of collective action. You're also friendly and enjoy companionship. You won't ally yourself with just anyone, though; you quickly size up people to determine who can benefit you and who'll drag you down. The hyena's distinctive "laugh" symbolizes your eagerness to communicate, but you can be abrasive or tactless and might need to learn to express yourself diplomatically.

Strengths: Discernment, sociability, originality

Weaknesses: Abrasiveness, rudeness, tendency to snap at others

How to use this animal's power: If you feel pressured into following rules or behaviors that aren't comfortable for you, a hyena can teach you how to get along with other people without compromising yourself. A hyena can also help you be more discerning.

Symbolic meanings: If a hyena appears to you in the waking world or a dream, it can mean you need to exercise discrimination and not allow devitalizing influences into your life. A hyena's appearance in your life may advise you not to lose your individuality in order to be accepted by others. It can also warn you to be more tactful and less argumentative.

Jaguar

Characteristics: Known for your grace and beauty, you often dazzle those with whom you come in contact, who admire your many physical gifts. Your lovely image, however, can belie your fierceness and ambition, and you might use your attractiveness to get what you want. Your keen intuition and perception also help you succeed by letting you see what others miss. You pursue your objectives with speed, strength, and stealth, and when you attack, you act swiftly and silently. Highly independent, you prefer to do things your own way and resent interference or direction from others. You have your own ideas and style, and no one had better try to change you.

Strengths: Beauty, grace, strength, stealth, intuition, independence

Weaknesses: Manipulativeness, stubbornness, antisocial behavior, aggressiveness

How to use this animal's power: This spirit animal can show you how to make the most of your appearance and to win the admiration of others. It can also teach you how to charm people in order to get what you want. If you've allowed other people to manipulate or dominate you, ask a jaguar to help you become more independent and confident.

Symbolic meanings: If you see a jaguar in real life or a dream, it might indicate that you're not using your physical gifts to their full potential. Or, it may suggest you're relying too much on outward appearances and need to turn within to connect with your inner beauty and strength.

Kangaroo

Characteristics: Like your totem, you easily leap over obstacles and jump out of harm's way. You bound ahead energetically when pursuing your goals, and don't turn back. However, you need a solid foundation from which to operate, or you may bounce around from one thing to another restlessly. This animal's large feet represent connection with the earth, and if this is your totem, it's important for you to stay grounded. Home and family can provide this stability for you, and you devotedly nurture your loved ones. You might even use your caretaking qualities in your job, perhaps in a health-related field.

Strengths: Balance, speed, stamina, ability to escape problems, faith in the unknown

Weaknesses: Inconsistency, restlessness, lack of focus

How to use this animal's power: When you must leap ahead into the unknown, ask a kangaroo to guide you. Invite this animal to show you how to bound over blockages and problems, so they don't impede your forward motion.

Symbolic meanings: If a kangaroo appears to you in the here and now or a dream, it may advise you to leap over a problem instead of trying to battle it head on. Kangaroos only move forward, so this animal might tell you to get hopping and jump ahead instead of hanging back. Sometimes a kangaroo's appearance signals an upcoming change.

Koala

Characteristics: Gentle and peace loving, you behave in a kind, compassionate way toward others and rarely say anything hurtful. You try to see the best in everyone and in every situation, refusing to focus on the harsh realities of life. As a result, you can sometimes be overly idealistic and naive. The koala lives in the treetops, which symbolizes a search for higher knowledge and spiritual truths. If this is your totem, you hold lofty goals and climb above earthy concerns and struggles.

Strengths: Gentleness, serenity, optimism,

Weaknesses: Naiveté, idealism, oversensitivity

How to use this animal's power: A koala can show you how to shift your perspective from one of negativity and skepticism to one of optimism and hope. It can also help you live a more peaceful life, away from the stress and struggles of the mundane world. Would you like to learn more about spiritual subjects? Invite a koala to teach you.

Symbolic meanings: If you see a koala in the waking world or a dream, it could advise you to retreat from challenges to a calmer, quieter place. It may recommend balancing the spiritual and material sides of your life. This animal's appearance might also warn that you're being too naive, and need to get your head out of the clouds.

Lion

Characteristics: The lion symbolizes leadership and royalty, and if this animal is your totem you probably feel comfortable at the head of a company, organization, or community. You won't be content in a subservient role, and enjoy being the center of attention. You are sociable, and family and community are important to you. You're protective and affectionate toward loved ones, and may tend to spoil your children. If challenged, you'll fiercely defend your position; however, you prefer to avoid conflict whenever possible—you're a lover, not a fighter. In a lion pride, the female does most of the work, hunting and raising the young; women who successfully balance careers and domestic duties may therefore have this animal as a totem.

Strengths: Leadership ability, strength, loyalty, sociability

Weaknesses: Laziness, pride, self-centeredness

How to use this animal's power: A lion can teach you how to live harmoniously with others. If you wish to play a more dominant or highly visible role, call upon a lion to show you how to grab the spotlight. Are you trying to handle the challenges of a job and family? Ask a lioness to lend you her power.

Symbolic meanings: If you see a lion in nature or a dream, it may tell you to take the lead and show your stuff: it's time to roar. A lion's appearance can also advise you to be more sociable, or, conversely, point out that you're spending too much time hanging out with friends instead of working and tending to other responsibilities.

Llama

Characteristics: Larger than its relative the alpaca, the llama hails from the heights of the Andes Mountains. Like this animal, you may climb to great heights, using your strength and endurance to achieve success. You willingly shoulder burdens and responsibilities and work hard to accomplish your objectives. However, you tend to take on more than your share and "carry the weight of the world on your shoulders." You persevere even under difficult circumstances, but if pushed too far you'll dig in your heels and refuse to go any further. If attacked, you defend yourself forcefully and aggressively protect those you love.

Strengths: Endurance, determination, responsibility, ambition

Weaknesses: Stubbornness, aggressiveness, inability to delegate responsibility

How to use this animal's power: A llama can show you how to skillfully tread a difficult path or to reach the heights to which you aspire. If you must shoulder a heavy burden, ask a llama to lend you its strength.

Symbolic meanings: If you see a llama while awake or dreaming, it might warn you to make sure you're on sound footing. It can also advise you to take it slow and steady, and stay balanced. A llama's appearance could mean you're trying to do too much or being too stubborn.

Manatee/Dugong

Characteristics: Trusting, open, and friendly, you readily extend yourself to others and bare your soul to those with whom you're close. However, your gentle nature and sensitive emotions can leave you vulnerable to less scrupulous types, and you usually feel most comfortable with a few close friends rather than large groups. Instead of rushing around and getting all stressed out, you prefer to move at your own, leisurely pace. You dislike conflict and competition, and in the workplace seek a position that doesn't involve too many deadlines or demands.

Strengths: Friendliness, gentleness, compassion

Weaknesses: Gullibility, oversensitivity, laziness

How to use this animal's power: If you've been pushing yourself too hard, ask a manatee to show you how to slow down and pace yourself. Are you the type of person who builds walls around yourself? If so, a manatee can teach you how to let down your guard and be more trusting. Ask for its assistance if you're taking care of children or the elderly.

Symbolic meanings: If you see a manatee in real life or a dream, it might recommend that you slow down and take it easy. On the other hand, if you've been procrastinating, a manatee's appearance may tell you to get moving. It can also warn you not to be so trusting or open.

Mink

Characteristics: People are often initially attracted to you for your beauty, but once they get to know you, they appreciate your friendly personality and cleverness as well. Sociable and playful, you enjoy all sorts of games, especially those that involve mental challenges. Your curious nature and quick mind lead you to explore a wide variety of interests, and you have trouble sticking with one thing for long. Perhaps you'll pursue a number of different careers during your lifetime, although jobs that use your communication skills would suit you best. Balancing mind and body could be one of your challenges in life.

Strengths: Beauty, mental agility, communication skills, playfulness

Weaknesses: Inconsistency, impracticality, talkativeness

How to use this animal's power: A mink can show you how to lighten up and have fun. If you've become stuck in a rut, ask a mink to guide you to new interests or activities. A mink can also help you improve your communication skills or learn a new subject.

Symbolic meanings: If you see a mink in waking life or while dreaming, it might remind you to be more playful. A mink's appearance may tell you not to rely on your looks alone. It could also encourage you to change your present course, either to expand your horizons or to avoid danger.

Mole

Characteristics: Quiet and clever, you know how to get into and out of tight spots without attracting attention. As a result, you can go undercover to gain hidden information or discover secrets. You burrow beneath the surface to learn the truth instead of being satisfied with superficial explanations. Intrigued by the hidden realms of the psyche, you might probe deep into your own inner wisdom or pursue a career in psychology. Your sensitivity and intuition enable you to understand things other people miss. People with a mole totem sometimes have poor vision, but your sense of touch is highly developed.

Strengths: Sensitivity, intuition, cleverness, persistence, inner wisdom

Weaknesses: Secretiveness, deception, blindness to truth

How to use this animal's power: When you feel closed in by darkness and difficulties, ask a mole to guide you to the light at the end of the tunnel. If you're seeking information about someone or something, a mole can help you to unearth it. A mole can also help you work with people who have vision problems.

Symbolic meanings: Seeing a mole in real life or a dream may mean that you're not seeing something you should—open your eyes. A mole could also advise you to dig deeper to discover the truth. Its appearance might warn that there's a "mole" in your presence.

Monkey

Characteristics: Playful and curious, you never lose your childlike sense of wonder and can always find a way to have fun. You're known for your intelligence and ability to learn new skills quickly. You also like to share ideas with other people and tend to be quite talkative—it's hard for you to be still or to keep a secret. A jokester, you enjoy playing tricks on people and mimicking them in a humorous way. You're a natural comedian and actor and often shine as the life of the party. With your dexterity and agility, you could also be an excellent athlete and might excel at gymnastics in particular.

Strengths: Intelligence, curiosity, playfulness, communication skills, sense of humor, agility

Weaknesses: Trickery, inconsistency, talkativeness, indiscretion

How to use this animal's power: If you're going through a dark and dreary period, ask a monkey to lift your spirits and show you how to have fun again. A monkey can also help you learn a new skill or subject, or to hone your communication skills.

Symbolic meanings: If a monkey appears to you when you're either awake or asleep, it might advise you to stop "monkeying around." If you've been working too hard, however, it could encourage you to lighten up and play more. Sometimes a monkey shows up to warn you that you're being tricked.

Moose

Characteristics: Despite your strength and impressive appearance, you don't try to dominate others or attempt to force your way in situations. You usually prefer to blend into the background instead of attracting attention to yourself. This trait can serve you well because other people often underestimate you, enabling you to go about your business undisturbed. You tend to rely on your own abilities rather than allying yourself with others. You're basically a loner and may feel awkward in social situations. Your well-developed senses let you quickly size up people and conditions, and you may be quite intuitive. The moose's huge antlers symbolize intellectual and spiritual power, which, combined with your physical resources, allow you to triumph over adversaries.

Strengths: Physical and mental power, self-reliance, keen senses, intuition

Weaknesses: Unsociability, awkwardness

How to use this animal's power: A moose can show you how to use your inner and outer resources to accomplish your objectives. When you don't want to attract attention, a moose can teach you how to keep a low profile.

Symbolic meanings: When you see a moose while awake or dreaming, it can warn you to camouflage yourself. It might also advise you to be more observant—use all your senses to assess what's going on around you. A moose's appearance might mean you're being too reclusive, or, conversely, that you need to withdraw for a while and become more self-reliant.

Mouse

Characteristics: Your quiet, shy, and unobtrusive nature leads you to seek a lifestyle that offers little stress or excitement. Because you tend to be sensitive and nervous, even timid, you don't like changes and often recoil from upsets of any kind. You feel most comfortable with steady routines, on the job and at home. A careful and dedicated worker, you usually prefer a subordinate role to one with a lot of visibility or responsibility. You enjoy curling up at home with a good book or spending time with your family, and may even be a bit of a recluse. You may have a tendency to hoard, like your mouse totem.

Strengths: Cleverness, adaptability, meticulousness

Weaknesses: Nervousness, timidity, possessiveness

How to use this animal's power: Call upon a mouse to help you appreciate the little things in life. Let this hard-working animal show you how to handle details and do things that require delicacy and dexterity. A mouse can also teach you the value of humility and modesty.

Symbolic meanings: If you see or dream about a mouse, it may mean that you're shutting yourself away and need to be more outgoing and sociable. Sometimes it warns you to be quiet and not draw attention to yourself. A mouse might appear when you need to stop wasting your energy, and eliminate the stress in your life.

Opossum

Characteristics: The opossum is noted for its tendency to "play dead," and if this is your totem you, too, know how to avoid danger by remaining quiet and still. You're also clever at assuming disguises or fooling others when necessary. Some of you may choose acting as a career, but regardless of whether you use this skill professionally you're capable of convincing people that you are what you claim to be. Like this animal, you have strong nurturing tendencies and can be very devoted to your loved ones. The opossum's pouch also symbolizes stored resources that you can draw on whenever you choose.

Strengths: Cleverness, acting ability, resourcefulness

Weaknesses: Deceit, trickery, pretension

How to use this animal's power: An opossum can teach you how to be quiet and still in order to escape harm or unwanted attention. If you want to put on a convincing show or keep up appearances, ask an opossum to lend you its acting power.

Symbolic meanings: If you see an opossum in the here and now or a dream, it may tell you that someone is trying to fool you. Conversely, it might warn you to "play dead" for a while until danger passes. This animal's appearance could also advise you to reach into your bag of tricks and pull out what you need to succeed.

Otter

Characteristics: No matter what your age, you maintain your childlike sense of wonder and have a playful, fun-loving nature. As a result, you attract plenty of admirers and probably maintain an active social life. You may love the water and enjoy swimming, boating, and other water sports. Despite your friendly personality and devotion to loved ones, at heart you're an independent person and don't like to be tied down. You have a curious streak and adapt easily to changes; you're always eager to try something new.

Strengths: Congeniality, playfulness, optimism, adaptability

Weaknesses: Rebelliousness, inconsistency, childishness

How to use this animal's power: When you feel discouraged or unhappy, call upon an otter to help you lighten up and have fun. If too many responsibilities are weighing you down, an otter can show you how to balance work with play. This spirit animal can also help you adjust to changes in your life.

Symbolic meanings: If you see an otter while awake or dreaming, you probably need to play more and enjoy life. This animal might encourage you to see things through the eyes of a child and be open to new adventures. If you've become stuck in a rut, an otter's appearance could mean that you need to make some changes.

Ox

Characteristics: Like your totem, you possess strength and endurance, and can shoulder heavy burdens without collapsing. Hardworking, patient, and persistent, you move through life in a slow, steady manner, believing in yourself and trusting that you will eventually get where you want to go. You don't hold great expectations, nor do you complain about the hand fate dealt you. A responsible member of your community or company, you always "pull your own weight" and seek the best for all concerned.

Strengths: Physical power, determination, patience, acceptance, responsibility

Weaknesses: Stubbornness, dullness

How to use this animal's power: When you need extra strength to keep going during hard times, an ox can give you the power you need. If you're embarking on a long-term project, ask an ox to teach you patience and perseverance. An ox can also help you to accept the burdens placed on you, without resentment or self-pity.

Symbolic meanings: If you see or dream of an ox, it could mean you aren't pulling your weight, or, conversely, that you're doing more than your share and need to delegate responsibility to others. If you're in the midst of an emotional situation, an ox may advise you to hold steady and take it one step at a time.

Panda

Characteristics: You have the ability to balance polar opposites in life—yin and yang (feminine and masculine) energies, give and take, rest and activity—as represented by your totem's black-and-white coloring. Balancing your own light and dark sides is also part of your life lesson. You're interested in both practical information and spiritual knowledge. Gentle, peace loving, and good-natured, you're most comfortable with a reclusive and solitary existence free of turmoil and can be content to just sit back and watch the world go by.

Strengths: Balance, gentleness, serenity

Weaknesses: Aloofness, lack of initiative

How to use this animal's power: A panda can teach you how to balance your own light and dark sides without judgment or self-criticism. In challenging circumstances, a panda can help you detach and observe things from a dispassionate perspective, in order to see more clearly.

Symbolic meanings: Seeing or dreaming of a panda might warn against viewing things in black and white—this isn't the time for extreme views or behavior. When a panda shows up, it urges you to bring harmony and balance to a situation instead of taking one side or the other. It can also tell you not be fooled by outer appearances.

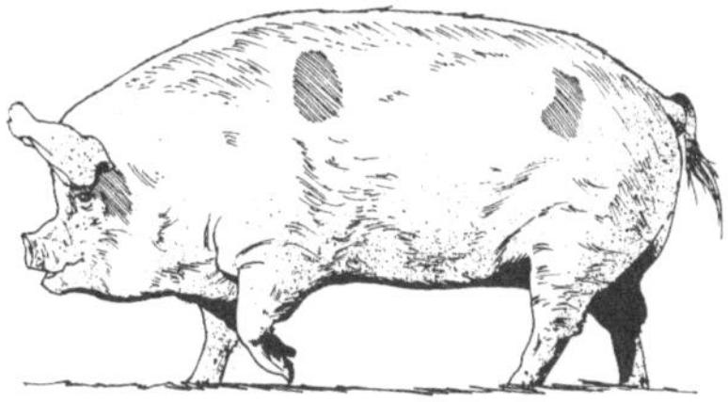

Pig

Characteristics: According to the Chinese zodiac, pig people are honest, good-hearted, intelligent, and cheerful individuals. You display generosity and hospitality to friends and strangers alike. In return, the universe blesses you with abundance and material goodies of all kinds—think about the piggy bank where money is stored. You can be indulgent, however, and may "pig out" on food, sex, or other sensual pleasures. At times, you might "hog" available resources instead of sharing. Some of you might need to pay more attention to housekeeping or personal hygiene.

Strengths: Honesty, congeniality, generosity, prosperity

Weaknesses: Indulgence, laziness, greed, uncleanliness

How to use this animal's power: A pig can teach you how to prosper financially by dealing honestly and fairly in business. If you tend to hoard your resources, a pig can encourage you to be more generous.

Symbolic meanings: If you see a pig in real life or a dream, it might advise you to watch your diet. Are you taking more than your fair share by hogging goods, money, or attention? Sometimes a pig's appearance can symbolize a need to clean up your act. A pig might also point out that you're wallowing in self-pity.

Polar Bear

Characteristics: Courageous and powerful, you brave conditions that might destroy less formidable folks. You know how to survive in harsh environments and rely on your own skills and initiative. Although blessed with abundant resources, you don't waste them. Instead, you manage what you have to safeguard yourself against hard times. Not only can you deftly handle physical challenges, you can also navigate the tricky waters of the emotional landscape with grace and inner strength. The polar bear's white fur represents a pure spirit: throughout your life, you strive to be true to yourself and to live in harmony with the universe.

Strengths: Physical power, courage, endurance, survival skills, emotional balance

Weaknesses: Aggressiveness, antisocial behavior

How to use this animal's power: When life seems bleak and forbidding, ask a polar bear to show you how to survive in the face of adversity. If you need courage to confront a challenge or to attack a problem, a polar bear can lend you its strength. A polar bear can also teach you how to be strong during physical or emotional trials.

Symbolic meanings: If you see a polar bear in the waking world or a dream, it might tell you to "bear up" during a period of difficulty or barrenness. Rely on your own resources, rather than on other people. A polar bear's appearance can also mean you're being cold emotionally, or that someone else's feelings have cooled.

Porcupine

Characteristics: Curious and trusting, you possess a childlike wonder that lets you find delight in many areas of life. Most of the time you're a good-natured sort, but when you feel annoyed or threatened you get prickly. Other people may underestimate your ability to defend yourself, for you don't appear strong or aggressive. However, with your sharp wit, you know how to sling barbs at your opponents and aim for their most vulnerable spots. You can also be overly critical of others and overly sensitive to what you perceive as criticism of you.

Strengths: Cheerfulness, curiosity, good defenses

Weaknesses: Sarcasm, hurtfulness, prickliness

How to use this animal's power: A porcupine can show you how to win an argument by cleverly getting the best of your opponent. It can also help you defend yourself from more powerful adversaries.

Symbolic meanings: If you see or dream of a porcupine, it might advise you to be less prickly and defensive. On the other hand, it might warn you to defend yourself or tell you that an attack is likely in the future. A porcupine may also show up to encourage you to be more curious and seek out life's pleasures.

Rabbit

Characteristics: You possess both mental and physical agility, and can shift gears quickly when necessary. Your speed enables you to beat others, whether on the playing field or in the boardroom, and to outwit your enemies. However, your restless nature makes it hard for you to stick with anything for long, and you rarely make long-term commitments. Gentle and affectionate, you're a lover not a fighter, and you can be flirtatious. Rabbits are also known for their fertility, and if this animal is your totem you might produce many children of the mind, as well as of the body.

Strengths: Speed, adaptability, creativity

Weaknesses: Inconsistency, irresponsibility, fickleness

How to use this animal's power: If you're beginning a creative venture or seek inspiration, invite a rabbit to help you get started. If you want to run circles around your competition, take a cue from a rabbit. A rabbit can also show you how to handle conflicts peacefully and to be less combative.

Symbolic meanings: Seeing a rabbit in waking life or a dream can mean you need to pick up the pace in some area of your life. It could also advise you to stop hopping from one thing to another. Sometimes a rabbit's appearance predicts a pregnancy or inception of a creative project.

Raccoon

Characteristics: People who have the raccoon as a totem can succeed at anything they undertake. Ingenious and resourceful, you have a knack for figuring out ways to deal with challenges and can readily adjust to changes—you don't let problems get you down. Instead, you apply your innate curiosity to find clever solutions. Like the raccoon, you might use your hands in skillful ways, from knitting to carpentry. You are known for being neat, clean, and organized; however, you might be a bit germ phobic. Although you're usually friendly and gentle, you can react fiercely when you feel threatened.

Strengths: Cleverness, resourcefulness, adaptability, orderliness

Weaknesses: Fastidiousness, sneakiness, nosiness

How to use this animal's power: Is clutter interfering with your efficiency? Ask a raccoon to help you get organized and become more productive. A raccoon can also show you how to clear up confusion or solve a baffling problem.

Symbolic meanings: The presence of a raccoon in real life or a dream might be advising you to use your skills and resources more effectively. This animal's appearance can also mean you need to clean up your act in some way. Perhaps you should stop hiding behind a mask and be more open and outgoing.

Ram

Characteristics: Like your totem animal, you possess strength and courage, and you use these qualities to climb to great heights. You thrive on competition and rarely back down from a challenge. Perhaps you have natural athletic ability or enjoy sports. In Western astrology, the ram is the symbol of Aries, the first sign of the zodiac, and many people with the ram as a totem are pioneers, inventors, or adventurers who eagerly strike out into new territory. You tackle problems head on and are known for your directness. However, you sometimes bang your head stubbornly against walls and refuse to try other tactics or acknowledge defeat.

Strengths: Courage, daring, physical strength, athletic ability, forthrightness, pioneering spirit

Weaknesses: Combativeness, aggressiveness, stubbornness

How to use this animal's power: When you need to forcefully face a problematic situation or person, ask a ram to give you the strength and courage to succeed. If you have trouble asserting yourself, a ram can teach you how to use your power. Invite this animal to join you in any type of competition.

Symbolic meanings: If you see a ram in real life or a dream, it could advise you to tackle a matter head on. Perhaps you need to engage an adversary forcefully and directly. A ram's appearance might also presage the beginning of something new.

Rat

Characteristics: Your ability to adapt and make the best of whatever situation you find yourself in serves you well in both personal and professional areas. You're also intelligent, ambitious, and shrewd, and, like the rat in Chinese astrology, you can achieve success in whatever you attempt. Sociable and cooperative, you understand the importance of teamwork. Many people with the rat totem are good managers because they know how to use the skills and talents of their employees to everyone's benefit. People sometimes mistrust you, but those who know you value your resourcefulness and lack of pretense.

Strengths: Adaptability, intelligence, shrewdness, resourcefulness, sociability

Weaknesses: Restlessness, destructiveness, slyness, nervousness

How to use this animal's power: Call on a rat for guidance when you need to learn something quickly. A rat can also show you how to use your intelligence and skills advantageously, especially in business. Let this animal teach you how to adapt to difficulties and survive against the odds.

Symbolic meanings: When you see a rat in the waking world or a dream, it could warn you that a rat is lurking in your presence or that someone is about to "rat" on you. This animal's appearance might also urge you to be shrewd in a business deal or financial venture. In some instances, this may mean cooperating with others or making use of their talents.

Reindeer

Characteristics: Your strength and endurance enable you to thrive even in harsh conditions. When faced with a physical or mental challenge, you buckle down and meet the task head on. A hard worker, you willingly shoulder responsibilities and can accomplish virtually anything you set out to do. You pursue your objectives with determination, and work well with others. However, you sometimes get stuck in a rut—it's important to change your direction from time to time and keep moving, in order to be happy and fulfilled.

Strengths: Persistence, endurance, responsibility, physical power, resourcefulness

Weaknesses: Workaholism, self-limiting behavior

How to use this animal's power: If you're beginning a task that will take a long time to finish, ask a reindeer to lend you its strength and determination. A reindeer can also help you shoulder heavy burdens and responsibilities. During periods of hardship, a reindeer can teach you how to endure and discover untapped resources.

Symbolic meanings: If you see or dream of a reindeer, it might advise you to address a challenge head on. Sometimes a reindeer appears when you're taking on a big responsibility; it encourages you to persevere. Hang in there! You can handle it. It might also tell you to keep moving; don't limit yourself and your options.

Rhinoceros

Characteristics: Because the origin of the rhinoceros dates back to the age of now extinct large mammals, people with this totem are often interested in history, anthropology, past lives, and ancient wisdom. The rhino's most notable feature—its horn—symbolizes sensitivity and insight. With your highly developed awareness, you can discern what's best for you in order to survive and succeed where others fail. You don't need to rely on other people's advice or experience; you can look within yourself for guidance. Basically solitary, you feel comfortable in your own skin and with your own ideas.

Strengths: Intuition, inner wisdom, self-reliance, discrimination

Weaknesses: Lack of trust, aloofness

How to use this animal's power: The rhino can show you how to use the lessons of the past to benefit you in the present. It can also teach you how to trust your own inner wisdom and rely on yourself instead of others. If you need to make a decision, ask a rhinoceros for assistance.

Symbolic meanings: When you see a rhinoceros while awake or dreaming, it may advise you to turn within to discover your own truth—only you know what's right for you. Its appearance could also tell you to be more discriminating. Perhaps you need to examine something in your past.

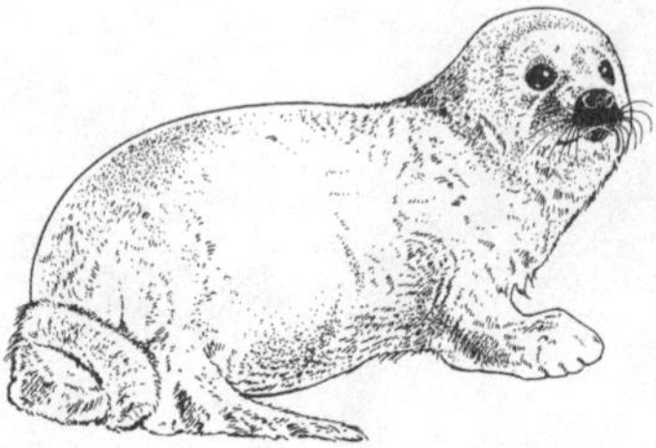

Seal

Characteristics: Water symbolizes intuition and imagination, so if this oceangoing mammal is your totem you are likely blessed with both qualities in abundance. You might also possess creative talent, as an artist, musician, or poet. Despite your sensitivity and dreaminess, you know how to bring your ideas down to earth and manifest them—just as the seal comes on land to birth its young. Agile and clever, you gracefully swim through emotionally upsetting situations, and can withstand harsh circumstances. You might even have the power to move between the worlds, or shapeshift like the legendary selkies (seal people) of Irish mythology.

Strengths: Imagination, intuition, creativity, endurance

Weaknesses: Dreaminess, impressionability, impracticality

How to use this animal's power: If you need inspiration to launch a new creative venture, invite a seal to assist you. This animal can also show you how to bring your ideas to fruition. A seal can guide you through an emotional crisis and help you stay balanced.

Symbolic meanings: Encountering a seal in a dream or waking life might advise you to pay more attention to your creative abilities and/or to put effort into developing your talents. Sometimes a seal suggests you're being too impractical, or, conversely, that you need to be more imaginative and not so pragmatic. A seal's appearance can also presage an emotional event.

Sheep

Characteristics: Unlike people whose totem is the ram, you have a gentle, docile, almost innocent nature. You dislike conflict or challenges, and quickly withdraw from situations you perceive as threatening, even if no danger truly exists. Sociable and family-oriented, you want to fit in and be liked. As a result, you may squash your individuality in order to please others. You tend to be a conformist and adopt the values and rules of your group. Accepting and tolerant of others, you make people feel at ease in your presence. You show compassion for those who are weaker than you, and may choose a career that involves caring for others.

Strengths: Compassion, gentleness, sociability, consideration for others

Weaknesses: Sheepishness, dependency on others, lack of imagination

How to use this animal's power: A sheep can show you how to be more innocent and childlike, to appreciate simple pleasures and recapture the joy of youth. It can also teach you how to get along harmoniously with others and how to avoid conflict.

Symbolic meanings: If you see or dream of a sheep, it might mean you feel vulnerable or weak. This animal may also encourage you to be gentler, more caring, or unassuming.

Skunk

Characteristics: Gentle, shy, and peace loving, you usually try to avoid conflicts and have few enemies. However, you don't run away from fights, either, and people who know you respect your bravery and ability to stand up for yourself. Your flexibility enables you to get along in most circumstances and to make the best of situations. For the most part, you feel confident about yourself and don't need other people's praise or social success to boost your self-esteem. Instead, you're a loner who prefers to plot your own course and steer clear of the maddening crowd.

Strengths: Confidence, courage, adaptability, modesty

Weaknesses: Defensiveness, arrogance, antisocial behavior

How to use this animal's power: If you feel you're being threatened, invite a skunk to help you stand your ground and defend yourself. A skunk can also show you how to be more self-confident and independent.

Symbolic meanings: When a skunk shows up in real life or a dream, it might be warning you to protect yourself or your assets. It could also mean you're letting other people intimidate you—maybe it's time to raise a stink about something you don't like. Sometimes, however, a skunk's appearance can signal you to withdraw from conflict rather than fighting back.

Snow Leopard

Characteristics: This rare and beautiful animal shares some qualities with jaguars and other leopards, but it is less aggressive. It also lives in the mountains rather than the jungles or plains. Like the snow leopard, you prefer a quiet, solitary life to one packed with people and excitement. Despite your grace, beauty, and sex appeal, you don't show off or try to attract attention, and tend to be quite shy. You pursue your goals without a lot of fanfare, using stealth instead of a direct frontal attack. Cautious and meticulous, you take great care in everything you do and thus avoid mistakes or setbacks. You likely possess keen intuition and an interest in spirituality.

Strengths: Beauty, sexual attractiveness, intuition, grace, precision

Weaknesses: Aloofness, skepticism

How to use this animal's power: When you want to go about your business without attracting attention, let a snow leopard show you how to maintain a low profile. Invite a snow leopard to accompany you on a spiritual retreat or guide you on an inner journey. This animal can also teach you the value of silence, and how to find comfort and peace in solitude.

Symbolic meanings: If you see a snow leopard in the waking world or a dream, it may mean you need to be quiet or to stay out of sight. It can also advise you to exercise care and sensitivity in a situation. Sometimes a snow leopard's appearance may herald a spiritual quest or experience.

Squirrel

Characteristics: Is your motto "be prepared"? If so, the squirrel could be your totem. Always alert and busy, you work hard to provide for yourself and make sure to "squirrel away" plenty, should hard times befall you. However, some people with a squirrel totem can be hoarders, afraid to part with anything. Despite your diligent nature, you still find time to play and are very sociable. You probably possess good communication skills and enjoy conversing with other people. Forward thinking, you spot trends and could be a wise investor. Like this animal, you may be nervous and high-strung, with a tendency to scatter your energy in too many directions.

Strengths: Resourcefulness, practicality, sociability, communication skills

Weaknesses: Stinginess, materialism, talkativeness, restlessness

How to use this animal's power: If you have trouble saving money, ask a squirrel for guidance. A squirrel might also help you make money through investments. This animal can teach you how to balance work and play.

Symbolic meanings: The appearance of a squirrel in real life or a dream could advise you to be more careful with your finances—don't spend everything you make. Sometimes a squirrel might warn that harder times lie ahead. This animal's appearance may indicate that you're working too hard and need to have more fun. It might also suggest that you're depleting your energy by trying to do too much.

Tiger

Characteristics: Like this splendid animal, you have a dynamic appearance and stand out in a crowd. You may be strong and large in size, but even if you're not physically impressive you possess amazing inner strength. When you want something, you pursue it fiercely and overpower your adversaries. Your courage, adventurous nature, and vitality attract many admirers, and you could be a strong leader; however, you usually prefer a solitary existence. You also exude sexuality and passion. Unlike many cats, tigers like water and swim well. Water symbolizes the emotions and intuition, so these qualities are well developed in people with this totem. Your feelings are easily aroused, and you can be unpredictable. The tiger's orange-and-black coloring links it with the full and new moons, and you may notice that your moods change according to the moon's phases.

Strengths: Beauty, power, courage, vitality, intuition, sensuality

Weaknesses: Aggressiveness, unpredictability, moodiness, antisocial behavior

How to use this animal's power: When you need courage and strength, call upon a tiger to lend you its power. If you're starting a new adventure, invite a tiger to accompany you. A tiger can help you beat out opponents in any type of competition.

Symbolic meanings: When you see a tiger in real life or a dream, it may advise you to be more assertive and to seek new adventures. If your life lacks passion, a tiger's appearance might suggest you need more excitement; conversely, it could warn you not to get swept away by your passions.

Unicorn

Characteristics: This mystical creature symbolizes purity, innocence, and faith in the rightness of the universe. Its single horn, which grows from the third eye or brow chakra, represents intuition and connection with the higher realms. If the unicorn is your totem, you possess exceptional intuition and can see beyond the physical world. You don't rely on intellect alone, you allow yourself to be guided by your inner wisdom and the higher forces. Your gentle nature is easily bruised by the harshness of everyday life, and, like your totem, you take flight when threatened or hurt. Interested mainly in spiritual things, you have trouble dealing with mundane matters and can tend to live in a fantasy world.

Strengths: Beauty, intuition, spirituality, inner wisdom, gentleness, purity, kindness

Weaknesses: Impracticality, flightiness, naiveté

How to use this creature's power: Let a unicorn help you connect with your intuition and inner vision. Ask this beautiful creature to take you on a shamanic journey and guide you into the spirit world. A unicorn can also teach you how to have faith during difficult times.

Symbolic meanings: If you see a unicorn in a dream or vision, it may tell you to keep the faith—don't give up. A unicorn could also advise you to be more gentle and kind. Encountering a unicorn might warn you to trust your intuition, not just your intellect.

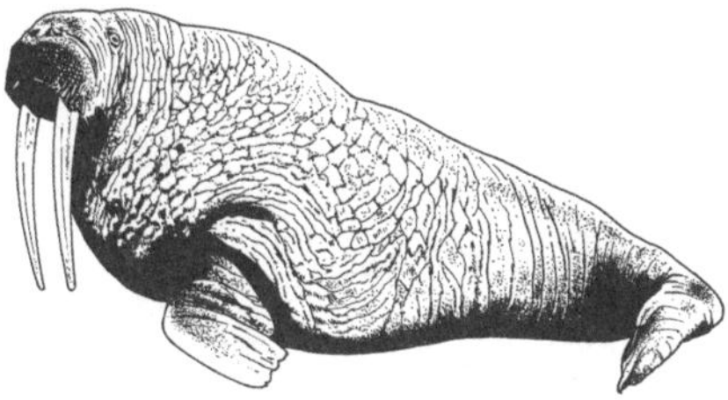

Walrus

Characteristics: Because the walrus lives both in the water and on land, people with this totem can navigate both physical and emotional situations comfortably. You're extremely sociable and community oriented—you need the company of other, like-minded individuals in order to thrive. The touchy-feely type, you enjoy physical contact and tend to be very affectionate with friends and family members. Strong and hardy, you possess good survival skills and can endure harsh conditions. Although you're usually easygoing, you can be a formidable opponent when someone threatens you or a loved one. Like the walrus, you dive deep into the mysterious realms to uncover secrets and hidden treasures. You might even have large teeth or sport a lush moustache.

Strengths: Physical power, hardiness, sociability, affectionate nature, protectiveness

Weaknesses: Dependence on others, lack of individuality, coarseness

How to use this animal's power: A walrus can show you how to get along with other people and to live harmoniously in your family or community. If you seek closer friendships or want to be more social, ask a walrus for assistance. This animal can also help you discover your hidden talents.

Symbolic meanings: If you see or dream of a walrus, it might suggest you need more contact with your own kind. On the other hand, it could mean you rely too much on other people and need to be more independent. If a walrus appears, ask yourself if you're being too thick-skinned.

Weasel

Characteristics: Known for your cleverness and ability to get out of difficult situations, you also have a knack for maneuvering yourself into positions of advantage. This is partly because you possess keen powers of observation, listening and watching other people closely to discover their secrets. You also know how to be quiet and to accomplish your objectives without revealing yourself. When threatened or angered, you attack fiercely. If someone crosses you, you'll "go for the jugular" and wound your adversary with cutting words or hurtful acts. Weasels eat up to half their own weight daily, so if this is your totem you might need to watch your diet.

Strengths: Ingenuity, observation skills, stealth

Weaknesses: Aggressiveness, spitefulness, slyness

How to use this animal's power: If you feel trapped by a situation, ask a weasel to help you find a way out. It can also show you how to get into places or groups that have shut you out. This animal can help you uncover secrets or understand other people's motives.

Symbolic meanings: When you spot a weasel in the waking world or a dream, it may warn you to be more observant. Protect yourself; someone might try to attack or undermine you. A weasel's appearance could mean you aren't being honest about something, or that another person is being dishonest with you. This animal may also advise you to watch what you eat.

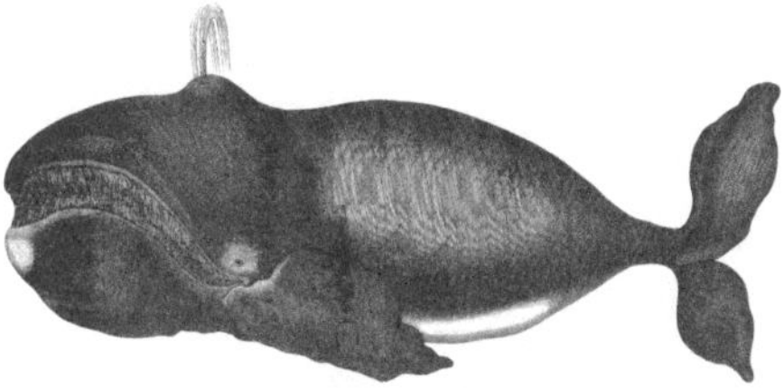

Whale

Characteristics: The whale is the largest of all mammals, and if it's your totem you, too, might be physically large and strong. However, you move with surprising grace and agility. Like the whale, you plunge into the depths—including your own psyche—to discover what lies beneath the surface. You possess keen intuition and insight, which can help you achieve your objectives. You're also creative and imaginative and might excel at singing or poetry. Because your totem lives in the ocean, which symbolizes the emotions, you're probably quite sensitive. At times you might feel emotionally overwhelmed or withdraw into yourself, but eventually you have to "come up for air."

Strengths: Insight, intuition, creativity, imagination

Weaknesses: Emotional instability

How to use this animal's power: Do you need help getting started on a new creative project? A whale can teach you how to dive deep within yourself for inspiration. A whale can also help you develop your intuition and use it effectively. Let this animal guide you through troubled waters.

Symbolic meanings: If a whale appears to you, whether you are awake or asleep, it may mean that you need to delve deeper into a situation. It might also encourage you to take a more creative approach or to use your creative abilities more productively. Sometimes a whale's appearance can presage an emotional event or experience.

Wolf

Characteristics: Like your totem animal, you have a wild and independent streak, but you're also quite sociable and affectionate, especially with close friends and family members. You're fiercely loyal to your loved ones and have a strong sense of community. Intelligent and intuitive, you are a natural leader and command the respect of your peers, but you're not usually arrogant or pushy. Although you possess strength and daring, you rarely attack unless you feel threatened.

Strengths: Intelligence, strength, loyalty, sociability

Weaknesses: Ritualistic, domineering, set in your ways

How to use this animal's power: A wolf can guide you in making appropriate choices in relationships of all kinds, and help you honor commitments to loved ones. It can also show you how to balance freedom and responsibility, sociability and independence. If you feel inadequate to a task, a wolf can give you strength and wisdom.

Symbolic meanings: If you see or dream of a wolf, it might advise you to use your strength and intelligence to protect the people close to you. If you have a tendency to be fickle or insincere, a wolf's appearance could suggest that you show more devotion and affection to your partner. A wolf can also tell you to be respectful of traditions and authority.

Zebra

Characteristics: The zebra's distinctive stripes allow it to hide from predators by blending into the herd. Like your totem, you may create an illusion to disguise yourself or your intentions. Your unique beauty and grace capture the attention of other people, and you probably have many admirers. Most of the time you're gentle, sociable, and protective of your loved ones. At times, though, you might feel that you are a combination of opposites, and one of your challenges in life is to balance the light and dark sides of yourself.

Strengths: Beauty, grace, balance, clarity

Weaknesses: Deception, tendency to lose yourself in the crowd, indecisiveness

How to use this animal's power: The zebra can help you see things more clearly. It can also show you how to prevent those who might harm you from seeing you clearly. Call upon a zebra to teach you how to balance opposing or competing factors in your life.

Symbolic meanings: If you see a zebra or dream about one, you may need to broaden your perspective instead of seeing things as simply black and white. This animal might show up when you're losing your sense of individuality and blending into the crowd. It could also warn you to protect yourself from enemies.

"Something about birds soaring through the air stirs our souls, motivating us to rise above our earthly concerns and learn more about a greater world beyond our Earth: the spiritual realm."

—Whitney Hopler, www.angels.about.com/od/MiraclesPopular-Culture/a/Birds-As-Divine-Messengers-Animal-Angels-Spirit-Guides-And-Totems.htm

BIRDS

Albatross

Characteristics: Resilient and determined, you know how to handle setbacks and recover from losses. Even though you may suffer hardships, you glean wisdom from all your experiences and grow stronger as a result of facing difficulties. You shoulder the responsibilities placed upon you and have the strength to tackle long-term projects without giving up. However, at heart you're a free spirit and hate being tied down. An eternal seeker, it might take you a while to discover your true purpose, and you'll likely continue searching for greater meaning and knowledge throughout your lifetime.

Strengths: Resilience, ability to bounce back from difficulties, determination, inner wisdom

Weaknesses: Flightiness, wanderlust, lack of direction, imbalance between mind and body

How to use this bird's power: If you feel burdened by responsibilities, ask an albatross to guide you through the hard times and free yourself. An albatross can also show you how to avoid succumbing to other people's expectations and chart your own course. If you need some good luck, call upon an albatross to assist you.

Symbolic meanings: If you see an albatross in real life or a dream, it may mean that even though things are difficult now, you'll soar above problems and grow stronger as a result of your experience. Sighting an albatross can mean good luck or a trip is in your future.

Blackbird

Characteristics: Many birds fly together in flocks, but not the blackbird. Like your totem, you're a loner and like to chart your own course in life. You might journey into territory others avoid or can't understand and may feel drawn to psychology or metaphysics. When others try to move into your territory, you protect it aggressively. Like the blackbird, you might have a lovely singing voice or other vocal skills—you could even use music or chanting as a healing tool. Certainly you possess many talents, and it's important to share these with the world.

Strengths: Creativity, musical talent, independence, healing powers

Weaknesses: Aggressiveness, aloofness, antisocial behavior

How to use this bird's power: If you wish to express your talents more fully or successfully, call upon a blackbird for assistance. Do you want to explore a spiritual path? Ask a blackbird to guide you. A blackbird can also help you perform well, whether you're on stage or in the boardroom.

Symbolic meanings: If you encounter a blackbird while awake or dreaming, it could advise you to break out of a rut and fly free. It might also encourage you to use your talents instead of hiding them away. Spotting a blackbird can mean you're in for a surprise.

Bluebird

Characteristics: Known as the bird of happiness, the bluebird is gentle and unassuming. If this is your totem, you have a kind and considerate nature, and try to avoid arguments or conflicts with other people. You focus on what's good in life rather than what's wrong, and possess a childlike ability to find pleasure in little things. You know how to enjoy yourself, and encourage other people to follow their bliss, too. Although you speak your own truth, you don't force your ideas on others, and instead show them how to be more content by being true to themselves.

Strengths: Happiness, inspiration, optimism, kindness, gentleness

Weaknesses: Naiveté, vulnerability

How to use this bird's power: When you feel "blue" and seek more joy in life, invite a bluebird to show you how to embrace happiness. A bluebird can teach you how to avoid conflict in life and how to live more harmoniously. It can also help you speak up for yourself without causing animosity.

Symbolic meanings: If you see a bluebird or dream about one, it reminds you to find more happiness in life. If you've been working too hard or shouldering heavy responsibilities, a bluebird urges you to enjoy yourself more. Sometimes a bluebird's appearance can be a sign of good luck or better times ahead.

Blue Jay

Characteristics: Fearless and assertive, you know what you want and don't hesitate to go after it. You refuse to let other people or obstacles stand in your way and hold your ground even when the odds are against you. However, you can be inconsiderate of others and might even bully weaker individuals or take advantage of them. The tuft on the jay's head symbolizes higher knowledge, and like your totem you may seek not only mundane knowledge but spiritual wisdom as well.

Strengths: Courage, assertiveness, determination, knowledge

Weaknesses: Aggressiveness, selfishness, lack of consideration for others

How to use this bird's power: This fearless bird can teach you how to be more courageous and daring. If someone is trying to push you around or steal your ideas, ask a blue jay to join you in chasing that person off. A blue jay can also help you pursue your objectives more aggressively.

Symbolic meanings: If you see or dream about a blue jay, it might advise you to be more assertive or to stand up for yourself. On the other hand, it could indicate that you're being too pushy or thoughtless. Sometimes a blue jay's appearance signals a time of intellectual or spiritual growth.

Canary

Characteristics: Your voice is one of your greatest assets, and using it correctly and advantageously could be one of your lessons in life. Like your totem, you might be an accomplished singer or songwriter. Or, you may excel at public speaking or other forms of communication. Your expressive skills can delight others, and you might even be interested in sound healing. At times, however, you can speak in a cutting or hurtful way, without considering the ramifications. Canaries are delicate and sensitive, and you might be especially prone to respiratory illnesses or throat ailments.

Strengths: Musical talent, communication skills

Weaknesses: Oversensitivity to colds/flu

How to use this bird's power: This beautiful songbird can teach you how to use your musical talent or voice more joyfully and productively. If you wish to communicate clearly with someone, ask a canary to show you how: a canary can help you sugarcoat your words so other people listen to what you say.

Symbolic meanings: If you see a canary in the physical world or in a dream, it might tell you to speak up and share your ideas with others. It could also encourage you to sing your own song, instead of mimicking someone else. Sometimes a canary appears to advise you to take better care of your health.

Cardinal

Characteristics: The cardinal's most notable feature is its vibrant red color. Like your totem, you're a colorful figure and brighten the lives of those with whom you come in contact. You easily command the spotlight and enjoy being the center of attention. You infuse everything you do with passion and vitality. Outgoing, hardy, and self-confident, you have a spirited nature and don't back down from challenges. You assert yourself enthusiastically and usually best your competitors. You have a strong nurturing side, too, and take good care of your loved ones—men with the cardinal totem make exceptionally good fathers.

Strengths: Vitality, enthusiasm, self-confidence, colorful personality

Weaknesses: Aggressiveness, arrogance, self-centeredness

How to use this bird's power: If your life seems dull and drab, invite a cardinal to enrich it with color and passion. A cardinal can teach you how to overcome nervousness, anxiety, or self-doubt, and become more self-confident and assertive.

Symbolic meanings: If a cardinal appears to you in the physical world or a dream, it might tell you to be more lively and spirited, and to enjoy life more fully. Don't hide in the shadows; show off your colors with flair. A cardinal's appearance could encourage you to be more passionate, or, conversely, warn you not to let your passions sweep you away.

Chickadee

Characteristics: With your cheerful manner and sociable nature, you easily attract people to you and probably have many friends and associates. One of the things people appreciate about you is your honesty. You share your ideas and opinions openly, but don't expect everyone else to agree with you. Most likely, you possess good communication skills and might choose a career that uses these. People sometimes underestimate you because you're so easygoing, and perhaps small in stature. However, you certainly aren't timid, and you self-confidently hold your own when challenged.

Strengths: Honesty, cheerfulness, friendliness, good communication skills

Weaknesses: Bluntness, indiscrimination

How to use this bird's power: This little bird can teach you how to win friends and influence people. If you tend to be overly critical of yourself or others, a chickadee can show you how to release judgmental behavior and be more accepting. When you need to say something you think others won't like, ask a chickadee to help you speak up with grace and tact.

Symbolic meanings: If you see a chickadee or dream of one, it may advise you to tell the truth or warn you that someone else might be dishonest. A chickadee's appearance could tell you to communicate information clearly and diplomatically, without arguing. It might also recommend openly sharing ideas with others.

Chicken

Characteristics: Because chickens lay eggs, they've long been associated with fertility and creativity. If this is your totem, you may express your creativity in many ways, from raising children to drawing to carpentry. You know how to bring your ideas down to earth and nourish the fruit of your imagination so that it can manifest. You generously nurture other people, both physically and mentally, and willingly help them to fulfill their potential. Strongly domestic, you create a safe and comfortable home for your family. However, you tend to fuss over your loved ones and can be overly protective of them. Of all the bird totems, the chicken is one of the most grounded; like it, you're a practical person not a dreamer.

Strengths: Creativity, fertility, nurturing nature, practicality, domestic skills

Weaknesses: Overprotectiveness, fearfulness

How to use this bird's power: Ask a chicken to help you nurture and birth a creative project. If you don't feel nurtured, call upon a chicken to take you under her wing.

Symbolic meanings: If you see a chicken in the physical world or a dream, it may advise you to use your resources creatively and nourish your gifts to bring them to fruition. A chicken can also predict the birth of something new. Sometimes a chicken's appearance is a play on words—you're being overly fearful or behaving in a cowardly manner; don't "chicken out."

Cockatoo

Characteristics: Innately caring and nurturing, you seek the best for everyone and share yourself willingly with those who need you—not just your immediate family, but people in your community, as well. To those you love, you are devoted and loyal. You also value your extended network of friends and associates and may belong to a number of groups. Your ability to offer words of encouragement and support could make you a good teacher, psychotherapist, minister, or physician. However, you sometimes speak in a harsh or blunt manner that can alienate the very people you wish to help.

Strengths: Caring nature, supportiveness, devotion, loyalty

Weaknesses: Outspokenness, raucousness

How to use this bird's power: A cockatoo can teach you how to communicate clearly and openly, especially with loved ones. It can also help you understand mixed messages or confusing situations with coworkers. When you're going through a difficult period with an elderly or sick person, ask a cockatoo to share its caregiver skills with you.

Symbolic meanings: If you see a cockatoo in the waking world or a dream, it could mean a misunderstanding will soon be resolved. Sometimes it advises you to be more supportive and caring toward someone you know, or may encourage you to take better care of yourself.

Condor

Characteristics: Like this high-flying bird, you soar to the heights and rise above difficulties and limitations. From your elevated perspective, you can see the big picture. Consequently, you have a broader and deeper understanding than most individuals. Your keen perception also gives you insight into other people and their motives. A condor symbolizes life, death, and rebirth. If this is your totem, you may have experienced many transitions in your lifetime, and those experiences have taught you how to make the best of bad situations.

Strengths: Insight, clarity, vision, perceptiveness

Weaknesses: Somberness, pessimism

How to use this bird's power: A condor can help you expand your vision and see beyond the ordinary details of day-to-day living. It can also teach you how to see deeply into other people and situations, in order to better understand them. If you're in the midst of a difficult transition, ask a condor to guide you to the other side.

Symbolic meanings: If you see a condor in the physical world or a dream, it could advise you to look more carefully at a person or situation. It may also encourage you to use patience and determination to rise above problems and obstacles. Sometimes a condor appears when a transition is imminent.

Cormorant

Characteristics: Like the cormorant, who dives deep into the water to catch its prey, you plumb the hidden depths to gain wisdom and insight. You have high ambitions, but not in the ordinary sense, and you long to be able to express your vision in a way that others will appreciate. It's likely your goals are of a metaphysical or spiritual nature, and you pursue them passionately—you want to bring light into the darkness. Perhaps you have artistic or musical talent. Even if other people doubt your ability to succeed, you believe in yourself and don't give up.

Strengths: Persistence, spirituality, wisdom, self-confidence

Weaknesses: Indulgence, stubbornness

How to use this bird's power: When you think something you desire is beyond your reach, a cormorant can show you how to push just a bit harder in order to grasp what you want. A cormorant can also help you follow your own unique path or to succeed in an unusual way.

Symbolic meanings: If a cormorant appears to you in real life or a dream, it may mean that you need to dive deep into the hidden realms—including your subconscious and the dream world—to discover important truths. A cormorant might also recommend immersing yourself in an emotional relationship or endeavor about which you feel passionately. Conversely, it could tell you to come up for air if your emotions are distorting your thinking.

Crane

Characteristics: You move in a graceful, balanced manner and, like the crane that engages in elaborate dance moves, you may be an excellent dancer. People admire you for both your beauty and your wisdom, for despite your age you seem to be an "old soul." Very private, you understand the value of silence and discretion. You don't need to show off or broadcast your opinions, which might expose you to attack. Like your totem, you can succeed at whatever you undertake because you know how to stay focused, conserve your energy, and pick your battles wisely. In Japan, cranes represent prosperity and longevity.

Strengths: Grace, balance, discretion, beauty, longevity

Weaknesses: Secretiveness, defensiveness

How to use this bird's power: If you're faced with a problem or dilemma, ask a crane to lend you its wisdom or teach you how to use your resources to find a solution. A crane can also help you focus on your goal and succeed at whatever you undertake. Ask a crane to show you how to balance mind, body, and emotions.

Symbolic meanings: If you see a crane while awake or dreaming, it might warn you to keep silent or be discreet. It could also advise you to conserve your resources and stay balanced. Sometimes a crane appears when good fortune is coming your way.

Crow/Raven

Characteristics: Known for your intelligence and communication skills, you enjoy learning new things and eagerly share your knowledge with others. You're also a keen observer and nothing much gets by you unnoticed; you might serve as an avatar or sentry. Some of you are interested in magic, ancient wisdom, and/or the occult. However, you tend to focus on the dark side and may be overly critical or suspicious. Family and friends are important to you and you are fearless when it comes to protecting them.

Strengths: Intelligence, vision, loyalty, vigilance, sociability

Weaknesses: Pessimism, aggressiveness, argumentativeness

How to use this bird's power: A crow can help you study for an exam, learn a new skill, or research information. If you're speaking in public, ask a crow to help you communicate effectively. Crow power can also enable you to get to the bottom of a murky issue or uncover a secret.

Symbolic meanings: If you see or dream about a crow, it could mean you'll soon receive a message. It might also advise you to speak up about something. Perhaps you need to stay alert to what's going on around you. Sometimes a crow's appearance signals deceit or betrayal.

Cuckoo

Characteristics: You take your time sizing up situations and go about your business in a slow, steady way. Instead of pressing for results, you allow matters to unfold at their own speed and thus minimize the chance of error. You believe in flowing with the current rather than struggling against it. As a result, you can readily adapt to changes and unexpected events. Your accepting attitude enables you to take advantage of opportunities, but you might also hang back and wait for good things to come to you rather than pursuing them. Cuckoos don't build their own nests, they move into other birds' homes. If this is your totem, you might depend on other people rather than relying on your own skills and initiative.

Strengths: Acceptance, adaptability, knowledge of natural rhythms

Weaknesses: Laziness, opportunism, dependency on others

How to use this bird's power: If you're launching a new venture or beginning a project, invite a cuckoo to help you proceed at the right rhythm. A cuckoo can show you how to go with the flow instead of getting stressed out.

Symbolic meanings: If you see a cuckoo while awake or dreaming, it could mean a change of residence is imminent. It might also warn you to listen carefully to what other people say. If you've been pushing too hard, a cuckoo could tell you to slow down. Sometimes a cuckoo's appearance is a play on words: you or someone else may be acting in a "cuckoo" manner.

Dove

Characteristics: The dove symbolizes peace, and, like your totem, you seek a tranquil existence free of stress and conflict. Known as a peacemaker, you help establish harmony between warring factions and might choose a career as a diplomat, mediator, or marriage counselor. Doves also represent love, and love is essential to your happiness. Deeply emotional, you shower friends, family, and romantic partners with love and devotion. Although the dove's distinctive song sounds mournful, this bird doesn't signify death. Rather, it brings hope and promise. You, too, maintain hope even during dark times and trust in the guidance of divine love.

Strengths: Loving nature, peacefulness, gentleness, optimism, spirituality

Weaknesses: Martyrdom, emotional imbalance, naiveté

How to use this bird's power: If you've suffered a painful loss, ask a dove to guide you through the hurt and release emotions that are holding you back. A dove can also help you resolve a dispute with someone and come to a peaceful reconciliation.

Symbolic meanings: When you see a dove in real life or a dream, or hear its mournful song, it tells you to mourn and honor people or things that have passed from your life, while also opening your heart and mind to the future. A dove's appearance can signal a time of peace. If you've had a disagreement with someone, it might encourage you to make peace with that person. A dove also urges you to be more loving.

Duck

Characteristics: Ducks can swim, fly, or walk on land, and people who have the duck as a totem tend to maintain a mind-body-emotion balance. You readily adapt to the situations in which you find yourself and usually handle changes without "getting your feathers ruffled." However, if things become difficult you may simply "migrate" to a different locale where life seems easier. Sociable and easygoing, you like to flock together with other people and probably have lots of friends or associates.

Strengths: Adaptability, sociability, emotional balance

Weaknesses: Inconsistency, tendency to go along with the crowd

How to use this bird's power: When you must make a big change that you find disconcerting, ask a duck to help you adjust comfortably to your new situation. A duck can also show you how to handle stress and establish balance in your personal and/or professional life.

Symbolic meanings: Seeing a duck in the waking world or a dream could mean a change is coming or that you need to be more flexible in some area of your life. A duck may also appear when you feel upset or stressed and need to establish better balance.

Eagle

Characteristics: Like this majestic bird, you soar high above earthly limitations and seek great heights, whether of a material or spiritual nature. From your elevated vantage point, you can see with clarity, and your broad vision allows you to understand what other people don't. You possess tremendous power, and learning to direct it constructively is one of your life lessons. A natural leader, you inspire others with your strength and independence. Once you've set your sights on a goal, you hunt it down with precision, speed, and determination. However, you may prey on those who are weaker than you and take advantage of them.

Strengths: Keen vision, precision, speed, spirituality, independence

Weaknesses: Predatory nature, ruthlessness, self-centeredness, opportunism

How to use this bird's power: If you've lost perspective on a situation, ask an eagle to help you see things more clearly. An eagle can show you how to pursue your goals with accuracy and vision. If you feel weighed down by responsibilities, let an eagle teach you how to soar above your problems and fly free.

Symbolic meanings: If you see an eagle in real life or a dream, it could advise you to see the big picture or look at a matter differently. It might also warn that you're not seeing something or someone clearly. An eagle's appearance can mean you need to pursue your quarry more forcefully. If you're immersed in material concerns, an eagle may urge you to be more spiritual.

Falcon

Characteristics: Like eagle people, you see with great clarity, keenly observing situations and people to ascertain the truth. Ambitious, you reach for the sky in your quest for either material or spiritual growth. You step back from the crowd to watch for opportunities, and when one arises, you seize it with speed and accuracy. You don't get bogged down in everyday details and duties; instead, you know how to soar above limitations and change your course quickly if necessary. A loner with a strong need for independence, you usually keep to yourself and might only let a few people get close to you.

Strengths: Keen observation skills, clarity, independence, spirituality

Weaknesses: Aloofness, opportunism, selfishness

How to use this bird's power: If you don't seem to be moving ahead fast enough, a falcon can point you toward a better path that will lead to your goals. Call upon a falcon to help you see and seize opportunities. This bird can also teach you how to be more independent.

Symbolic meanings: If a falcon appears to you in the waking world or a dream, it may advise you to take advantage of an opportunity quickly. If you feel trapped by responsibilities, a falcon urges you to rise above your limitations. Sometimes this means becoming more independent instead of getting wrapped up in other people's problems. A falcon might show up to warn you that you're not seeing something clearly.

Finch

Characteristics: People with the finch as a totem often have melodious voices, and you might be an accomplished singer or orator. A career in public speaking or music could suit you well. You use your excellent communication skills in networking and have a talent for promoting your ideas and those of other people, so marketing or public relations might also be good fields for you to pursue. The goldfinch totem, in particular, signifies happiness and good fortune; your positive attitude brings good things your way. Sociable and versatile, you can be found engaged in a wide variety of activities and interacting with many types of people. "Vive la différence" might be your motto.

Strengths: Adaptability, sociability, communication skills, versatility

Weaknesses: Talkativeness, indiscrimination, lack of focus

How to use this bird's power: Ask a finch to help you find your own voice and to express yourself better. If you want to expand your social network, call upon a finch to show you how to make connections. A finch can also teach you how to promote yourself and your talents successfully.

Symbolic meanings: Because many different types of finches exist, pay attention to the bird's coloring to interpret its meaning. A goldfinch could presage good luck; a purple finch symbolizes spiritual power. When a finch shows up in the physical world or a dream, it can mean a new opportunity or activity will soon come your way. A finch's appearance can also warn you to be careful what you say or to listen carefully to what other people say.

Flamingo

Characteristics: Sociable, outgoing, and good-natured, you enjoy the company of friends and family. Your colorful personality and attractive appearance draw others to you, and you probably have an extensive social network. You understand the meaning of teamwork and value the structure that comes from working with a group for a collective purpose. Good at organizing others, you willingly assume responsibilities, but you know how to delegate, too, and stay balanced as a result. You have the ability to sort out what's important and what's not, and use your analytical skills wisely in both personal and professional arenas.

Strengths: Discernment, congeniality, sociability, organizational skills, balance

Weaknesses: Dependence on others, pickiness

How to use this bird's power: Want to expand your circle of friends and colleagues? Ask a friendly flamingo to share its power of attraction with you and help you be more colorful. A flamingo can also teach you how to function well in a group or to bring people together for a cause. Let a flamingo show you how to balance work and play.

Symbolic meanings: If you see a flamingo while awake or dreaming, it could mean either you need to be more sociable, or, conversely, that you're spending too much time hanging out with friends. A flamingo's appearance might urge you to use discrimination. Sometimes a flamingo shows up when your life is out of balance.

Goose, Domestic

Characteristics: Like the goose, which is at home on land, in water, or in the air, you're quite versatile and adaptable. You have a number of diverse skills and talents, and can succeed in many areas of life. Not the least bit shy, you go after what you want and don't hesitate to speak your mind. You can be argumentative or boastful, however, and might not show respect for other people's opinions. Always alert to danger, you protect what you cherish—your property, loved ones, or ideas—with fierce determination.

Strengths: Protectiveness, courage, versatility

Weaknesses: Talkativeness, irritability, argumentativeness, aggressiveness

How to use this bird's power: When you need to stand your ground or protect yourself, ask a goose to assist you. A goose can also help you state your case, share ideas, or get your point across. If you must adapt to changing circumstances, a goose can show you the way.

Symbolic meanings: Seeing a goose in the real world or a dream may warn you to strengthen your defenses. It could also advise you to draw on your inner strength, not just physical resources. If you feel other people are taking advantage of you, a goose's appearance could tell you to stand up for yourself.

Grackle

Characteristics: The grackle's coloring can shift from black to green to purple, depending on how you look at it. If this is your totem, you, too, are adept at changing your appearance or presenting different images. This enables you to move in various circles and assume many roles. You could be an excellent actor or politician. Gregarious and talkative, you enjoy socializing and sharing ideas with others. However, you can become argumentative if someone "ruffles your feathers." Your emotions are easily engaged, and unless you learn to balance them, you risk depleting your energy through emotional upsets and excesses.

Strengths: Vocal skills, adaptability, versatility, sociability

Weaknesses: Argumentativeness, emotional imbalance, duplicity

How to use this bird's power: If you wish to make an impression on someone, ask a grackle to show you how to present yourself effectively. A grackle can also teach you how to express yourself more successfully. If you feel emotionally blocked, let a grackle help you connect with your feelings.

Symbolic meanings: If you see or dream of a grackle, it could warn you to examine something more closely; it might not be what it seems. A grackle's appearance may advise you to watch what you say. It can also tell you to stop wasting energy arguing and take action.

Grouse

Characteristics: The grouse is known for its unique dance-like movements, and if this is your totem you probably love to dance. You display natural rhythm in all your movements and might enjoy music, especially drumming. Quite likely, you're also sensitive to the rhythms and patterns of daily existence, and perhaps establish lots of little rituals that make you feel comfortable. When those patterns get upset, your "feathers get ruffled," and when you're annoyed you tend to "grouse" about people and situations. Learning to move smoothly with the ebb and flow of life is one of your challenges.

Strengths: Natural rhythm, grace, sensitivity

Weaknesses: Ritualistic behavior, irritability, tendency to complain

How to use this bird's power: If you like to dance, invite a grouse to be your partner and guide you gracefully across the floor. A grouse can teach you how to move in a more rhythmic and flowing manner. This bird can also help you adapt to the rhythm of life and learn to go with the flow.

Symbolic meanings: The presence of a grouse in the waking world or a dream could mean you're out of sync and need to get back into the rhythm of things. This bird's appearance might also tell you to stop "grousing" about something.

Gull

Characteristics: The gull spends most of its time in the water or air, but it also scavenges for food on land. Like your totem, you've learned to master the emotional, mental, and physical worlds and move easily between them. You know how to make the best of opportunities and adapt to conditions. Resourceful and clever, you use your keen powers of observation to assess situations and learn how to behave in various circumstances. You express your ideas openly and forcefully—other people know where you stand. However, they might find your outspokenness annoying at times.

Strengths: Versatility, adaptability, resourcefulness, intelligence

Weaknesses: Opportunism, bluntness, raucousness

How to use this bird's power: A gull can show you how to recognize opportunities and seize them quickly. It can also teach you how to size up people and situations, so you understand the rules of conduct. If you need to assert your opinions more aggressively, ask a gull to lend you its voice.

Symbolic meanings: If you spot a gull in real life or a dream, it may tell you to grab an opportunity before someone else does. A gull's appearance might also advise you to speak up about a particular matter. Seeing a gull can indicate a need to balance your body, mind, and emotions.

Hawk

Characteristics: Known for its vision, the hawk soars high into the sky to view the territory and spot its prey. Like your totem, you possess keen observation skills that enable you to see what other people miss. Your vision gives you the ability to spot trends, sense conditions, and even gaze into the future. As a result, you home in on opportunities and seize them. You reach for the heights and soar above the masses, achieving impressive success. Many of you seek to rise above the mundane world and pursue spiritual paths. You glean inspiration from the higher realms of consciousness and apply your insight to earthy endeavors, elevating whatever you do above the ordinary.

Strengths: Vision, insight, fearlessness, inspiration, precision, creativity

Weaknesses: Predatory nature, ruthlessness

How to use this bird's power: A hawk can give you insight into what's really happening and what's likely to transpire in the future. Ask a hawk to guide you in making decisions; it can show you the best course to take. If you're beginning a spiritual journey, invite a hawk to accompany you.

Symbolic meanings: If a hawk appears to you in the waking world or a dream, it may be telling you to open your eyes—you need to see something more clearly. A hawk might also encourage you to set your sights higher or to grasp an opportunity. Sometimes it appears when you're getting mired in everyday problems and urges you to rise above petty concerns.

Heron

Characteristics: This majestic bird wades through the water on long legs and uses its pointed beak to capture its prey. Like your totem, you deftly navigate emotional situations and reap rewards from your experiences. Your intuition enables you to spot and snatch what you want in life. A loner, you rely on yourself and don't need other people for support or guidance. Instead, you follow your own wisdom. When murky or unpleasant circumstances threaten to bog you down, you know how to spread your wings and fly freely above the muck.

Strengths: Independence, intuition, insight, versatility

Weaknesses: Aloofness

How to use this bird's power: If you need to be more independent, ask a heron to show you how to stand on your own. If you feel swamped by an emotional issue, a heron can teach you how to be more detached. Call on a heron to help you take advantage of opportunities.

Symbolic meanings: Seeing or dreaming of a heron may advise you to stand on your own two feet. A heron might show up when you're wading through an emotional situation to guide you safely. Its appearance could also advise you to balance body, mind, and emotions.

Hummingbird

Characteristics: Although the hummingbird is the smallest of all birds, it displays surprising fierceness when defending its territory. Like your totem, you aren't easily intimidated. Independent and adventurous, you have your own unique way of doing things. The hummingbird is attracted to red, the color of passion, and you pursue your objectives with passion. You drink deeply of life's nectar and in the process "pollinate" the world around you with joy and sweetness. Amazingly adaptable, you can change course quickly when circumstances require it. But you also know how to pause and observe a situation carefully before plunging in.

Strengths: Versatility, enthusiasm, creativity, self-confidence

Weaknesses: Inconsistency, aggressiveness, arrogance, indulgence

How to use this bird's power: Have you lost touch with joy and passion? If so, call upon a hummingbird to help you find life's sweetness again. A hummingbird could teach you about healing with botanicals through aromatherapy, flower essences, or herbal medicine.

Symbolic meanings: If you see a hummingbird waking or in a dream, it often suggests that you should look for the sweetness around you and pursue life with more passion. It could also advise you to take time to enjoy the flowers.

Kingfisher

Characteristics: This intriguing bird builds its nest along the banks of bodies of water, and if this is your totem you, too, prefer to live near an ocean, lake, or river. Kingfishers fly above the water and dive into it to catch fish. Therefore, this is often the totem of fishermen. Like this bird, you dive into experiences and aren't afraid to plunge headlong into situations in order to grab what you want. Your daring and hardiness enable you to go places and do things that might intimidate others. As a result, you can prosper by forging ahead into risky areas or by breaking new ground. You're also willing to delve deeply into your own subconscious—sometimes the most frightening territory of all—and discover what lies within.

Strengths: Adventurousness, emotional depth, hardiness, feminine power

Weaknesses: Recklessness, impulsiveness, emotional imbalance

How to use this bird's power: A kingfisher can give you the courage to "take the plunge" into a risky venture. If you're undergoing psychotherapy, ask a kingfisher to guide you into your own depths. This bird can also teach you how to overcome fear of emotional intimacy, especially if you've been hurt in the past.

Symbolic meanings: If a kingfisher appears to you in the waking world or a dream, it may recommend that you stop skirting the surface and dive deeper into a situation—be more daring. This bird sometimes appears when abundance is about to come your way. It can also advise you to pay more attention to your emotional life.

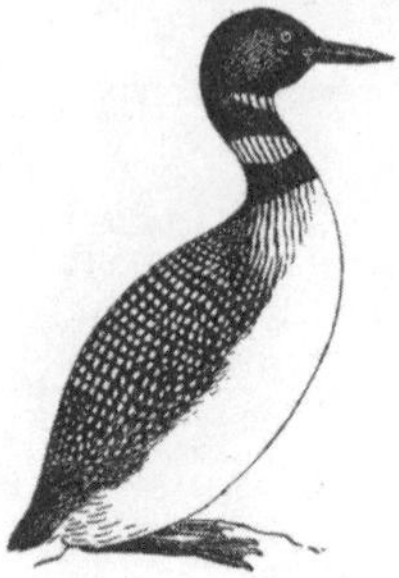

Loon

Characteristics: Loons can swim better than other birds and spend virtually all their time around water. Water symbolizes the unconscious, so if the loon is your totem you may dive deep into other levels of consciousness or move between the worlds as shamans do. Perhaps psychology or metaphysics interests you. Your imagination and intuition are highly developed; you might see visions, have vivid dreams, or be psychic. Your extraordinary sensitivity can make it difficult for you to be around other people, though, and you may choose a solitary existence. The loon's strange call represents an ability to communicate in unique ways or a desire to express unconventional ideas, perhaps of a mystical or occult nature.

Strengths: Intuition, imagination, shamanic power

Weaknesses: Oversensitivity, impracticality, aloofness

How to use this bird's power: A loon can guide you into the spirit realm and/or into altered states of consciousness. If you have trouble expressing your feelings, a loon can teach you how to connect with your emotions. Ask a loon to assist you in developing your intuition.

Symbolic meanings: If you see a loon in the physical world or a dream, it might warn you to use your intuition, not just your intellect. It can also advise you to dive beneath the surface to discover the truth. Sometimes a loon's appearance means you're letting your emotions cloud your thinking, or that you're living in a dream world.

Magpie

Characteristics: Magpies are opportunists, and, like your totem, you're very resourceful. When opportunities present themselves, you quickly seize them. You know how to make the best of any situation and can adapt to changing circumstances easily. Intelligent and versatile, you excel at problem solving. As a result, you can achieve success in any field of endeavor. Your pursuit of knowledge might lead you to investigate metaphysical subjects and to use magical knowledge or inner wisdom to guide you through life.

Strengths: Intelligence, resourcefulness, adaptability

Weaknesses: Opportunism, insensitivity to others, dishonesty

How to use this bird's power: Ask a magpie to help you learn a new subject or develop a skill, and then to apply it advantageously. If you're faced with a perplexing problem, a magpie can help you solve it. If you want to study occult knowledge, let a magpie take you under its wing and teach you its secrets.

Symbolic meanings: If a magpie appears to you in the waking world or a dream, it might advise you to use your resources wisely or more fully. This bird can also encourage you to take advantage of an opportunity or to make the best of something. Sometimes a magpie's appearance means something unexpected or unusual is about to happen.

Meadowlark

Characteristics: Like the meadowlark, you approach life with a cheerful and optimistic perspective. Even when things look bleak, you push on and refuse to let troubles crush your spirit. For the most part, you feel comfortable with yourself and don't try to be something more than you are. You speak your mind openly and live your own truth, without judging others. Your self-confidence comes partly from being in touch with both your inner and outer world. People who have the meadowlark as a totem often have melodious voices and enjoy singing.

Strengths: Optimism, cheerful disposition, self-confidence, balance

Weaknesses: Idealism

How to use this bird's power: If you've been going through a rough time, ask a meadowlark to show you how to reclaim your happiness and find joy in little things. A meadowlark can teach you how to speak your own truth and discover your self-worth.

Symbolic meanings: If you see a meadowlark while awake or dreaming, it heralds a time of improvement and happiness. Something new might be about to awaken in your life. This bird encourages you to seek joy and be hopeful. A meadowlark's appearance can also urge you to sing out, to express yourself honestly and confidently without worrying about other people's opinions.

Mockingbird

Characteristics: The mockingbird is known for its ability to mimic sounds, and if this is your totem you can learn languages easily; you might even speak several. Your gift for communication enables you to talk to people in their own "language" so that you can get your point across. Therefore, you could be a good teacher, writer, diplomat, or interpreter. You might also possess musical talent or acting ability. If you find yourself in a difficult or dangerous situation, you can usually talk your way out of it. Although you learn from other people's experiences and take what you find useful from them, you don't merely copy what others have done; you put your own unique spin on things.

Strengths: Communication skills, gift for languages

Weaknesses: Talkativeness, mimicry, duplicity, gossiping

How to use this bird's power: Do you want to learn a new language? Ask a mockingbird to tutor you. Invite a mockingbird to guide you if you're speaking in public, performing on stage, or making a presentation. A mockingbird can also help you improve your communication skills.

Symbolic meanings: If you see or dream of a mockingbird in nature, it encourages you to "sing" or speak out without fear of ridicule. Sometimes this bird's appearance advises you to express your originality instead of mimicking someone else.

Oriole

Characteristics: The oriole's black-and-orange coloring symbolizes balancing opposites: light and dark, positive and negative, masculine and feminine. If this is your totem, you know how to integrate the different parts of yourself and find balance. This enables you not only to be comfortable with yourself, but also to accept other people as they are. Contented and usually cheerful, you can establish pleasant relationships with others that offer mutual benefits. Your willingness to communicate clearly and honestly lets you work through challenges to create harmony. The oriole weaves its nest, and people with this totem may enjoy knitting, weaving, and other crafts.

Strengths: Balance, contentedness, relationship skills, ability to make connections

Weaknesses: Naiveté, sensitivity to cold

How to use this bird's power: An oriole can help you balance the light and dark sides of your personality. If you've experienced hard times lately, ask an oriole to guide you to happiness and teach you how to be cheerful again.

Symbolic meanings: Because the oriole is associated with approaching summer, its appearance signals brighter times ahead. If you spot an oriole in the waking world or a dream, it may recommend that you find more happiness within yourself and in the world around you.

Ostrich

Characteristics: One of the birds that cannot fly, the ostrich represents groundedness and a strong connection with the earth. If this is your totem, you know how to bring your ideas down to earth and apply them in practical ways. Most likely, you're interested in pragmatic areas and things that can benefit you in the material world. You keep your feet on the ground and don't get lost in fantasies. Although the ostrich can't fly, it can run fast, and like this bird, you may be a swift runner and enjoy sports that require speed. The ostrich's reputation for hiding its head in the sand (which it doesn't actually do) suggests that you might refuse to consider new ideas or unconventional approaches, or may ignore what's going on around you.

Strengths: Pragmatism, logical thinking, swiftness

Weaknesses: Lack of imagination, ignorance

How to use this bird's power: An ostrich can help you find practical applications for your ideas. It can also show you how to keep your feet on the ground during confusing or upsetting situations.

Symbolic meanings: If you see an ostrich while dreaming or in the waking world, it may warn that you're not paying attention to something you should—get your head out of the sand. An ostrich might also appear when you're out of touch with the world around you.

Owl

Characteristics: Owls, of course, are associated with wisdom, so if this bird is your totem, you're not only smart but wise as well. Perhaps you're interested in ancient or occult knowledge, or you might be something of a detective who hunts down hidden information and secrets. Your keen powers of observation enable you to see things other people miss. A loner and adventurer, you often prefer to go it alone, although you can be very devoted to the people you love. You might be a "night owl" and are at your best when the rest of the world sleeps.

Strengths: Intelligence, intuition, vision, accuracy

Weaknesses: Secretiveness, aloofness

How to use this bird's power: When you need to get to the bottom of a matter, ask an owl to help you see clearly and understand the truth. An owl can also help you pay attention to details and home in on what's important. Call on an owl to assist you in any endeavor that requires intelligence or insight.

Symbolic meanings: If an owl appears to you in the physical world or a dream, it can mean you need to open your eyes and pay closer attention to something. Its appearance might advise you to sharpen your mental skills or study harder. An owl may also warn you to be on the alert—something important is about to happen.

Painted Bunting

Characteristics: Eye-catching and distinctive, you turn heads wherever you go. Even when you aren't trying to attract attention, your exceptional beauty can't be hidden. You enjoy wearing brilliant colors, flashy clothing and jewelry, and imaginative makeup. Perhaps you dye your hair a dazzling hue—or several colors. Despite your theatrical appearance, you're really quite shy. You're not vain; you just enjoy the finer things in life. A career in the visual or performing arts could allow you to express your love of beauty and colorful nature creatively.

Strengths: Beauty, fashion sense, artistic ability, colorful personality

Weaknesses: Showiness, self-indulgence

How to use this bird's power: When you want to stand out in the crowd or make a big impression, ask a painted bunting to help you create an unforgettable look. A bunting can teach you how to express yourself in a more colorful or artistic manner. It can also inspire you to enjoy the beauty all around you.

Symbolic meanings: Seeing a painted bunting in real life or a dream can mean that you need more color and beauty in your life. It can also recommend that you pay more attention to your appearance: don't be afraid to be glamorous. Sometimes a bunting warns you not to be fooled by appearances.

Parrot

Characteristics: Like the parrot, you're extremely colorful and stand out brilliantly from the crowd. Whether or not you're physically beautiful, you have a majestic presence; you light up any gathering and your personality dazzles everyone who meets you. You can even get away with being outlandish at times. You love bright colors and like to dress in eye-catching clothes. Intelligent and sociable, you possess highly developed communication skills and enjoy discussing ideas with other people. A career in teaching, journalism, acting, or marketing could suit you well. You learn languages easily and may speak several, and might excel as a linguist or interpreter.

Strengths: Communication skills, colorful personality, intelligence

Weaknesses: Talkativeness, boisterousness, arrogance

How to use this bird's power: Want to make a big impression on someone? A parrot can show you how to attract attention. When you need to speak your mind, ask a parrot to help you find the right words to express yourself. If you want to learn a language, let a parrot tutor you.

Symbolic meanings: A parrot that appears to you in the waking world or a dream may tell you to be more colorful—don't blend into the crowd. A parrot could also urge you to express yourself loudly. Sometimes it may appear when you're merely "parroting" someone else instead of thinking for yourself.

Peacock

Characteristics: Your magnificent appearance awes everyone who sees you, and you never fail to attract attention wherever you go. Like the beautifully colored peacock, you wear dazzling colors and may dress in the latest fashions. Some of you could succeed as models, fashion designers, or actors. You like to "strut your stuff," however, and might be rather vain. In mythology, the peacock is often worshiped as a sacred creature; you, too, might seek adoration. Or, you may serve as a spiritual teacher or representative of a mystical organization. The eye-like designs on a peacock's feathers symbolize great vision, and you may have the power to see things other people miss.

Strengths: Beauty, style, colorful personality

Weaknesses: Vanity, arrogance

How to use this bird's power: When you want to appear glamorous and wow others, invite a peacock to teach you its beauty secrets. A peacock can show you how to stand out in a crowd or dazzle someone you're interested in.

Symbolic meanings: Seeing or dreaming of a peacock might advise you to dress up and look your best—don't hesitate to attract attention. Or, it could tell you to stop being so vain and exercise a little modesty. A peacock's eerie scream may warn you to pay attention.

Pelican

Characteristics: You understand the importance of teamwork and know how to cooperate with others in order to accomplish your objectives. Resourceful and practical, you can bring people together whose skills and talents complement each other. You don't feel a need to be a leader; you're content to serve in whatever capacity benefits the whole and you unselfishly offer your assistance to whoever needs it. A career in social services or a humanitarian organization could suit you well. One of your challenges, however, is to avoid getting involved in other people's problems and to balance your emotions with intellectual discernment.

Strengths: Compassion, unselfishness, resourcefulness, cooperation

Weaknesses: Martyrdom, lack of discrimination

How to use this bird's power: A pelican can show you how to work cooperatively and constructively with other people and to use your talents to serve humanity. If you tend to be arrogant or selfish, ask a pelican to help you develop more compassion and humility.

Symbolic meanings: A pelican might show up in the physical world or a dream when you're not paying enough attention to your own best interests. A pelican can warn you not to sacrifice yourself for someone else. During an emotional period, its appearance may suggest that you try to be more detached and discriminating.

Penguin

Characteristics: The penguin's ability to move easily between water and land symbolizes the power to slip between the waking and dreaming worlds. If this is your totem, you might even undergo out-of-body experiences. You can also navigate both the emotional and physical realms smoothly, and can successfully balance your personal and professional lives. The penguin's feathers resemble a tuxedo, and you might seem rather formal or cool. However, the black-and-white coloring also signifies your skill at integrating the dark/light, feminine/masculine sides of your personality. Both men and women with this totem are nurturing and protective, and make good parents.

Strengths: Balance, nurturing nature, intuition

Weaknesses: Dreaminess, emotional coldness, tendency to see things as black and white

How to use this bird's power: If you have trouble getting in touch with your emotions or your feminine side, ask a penguin to show you how it's done. A penguin can also teach you how to balance a career and family life.

Symbolic meanings: If you see a penguin in waking life or while dreaming, it could mean you need to balance mind and body—emotional upsets can lead to physical ailments. A penguin's appearance can indicate that you're opening up to new levels of awareness.

Pheasant

Characteristics: Like pheasants in the wild, you prefer open spaces and don't like being caged or fenced in. Your hardy nature and independence enable you to succeed even in challenging conditions. You're also the practical sort, and can excel at finding useful ways to apply your ideas. If the male pheasant is your totem, you may be rather dramatic and like to present yourself in a colorful manner. The female's plumage, on the other hand, enables her to conceal herself in her surroundings. If this is your totem, you know when to show off and when to keep a low profile.

Strengths: Independence, hardiness, practicality, self-preservation

Weaknesses: Vanity, lack of imagination

How to use this bird's power: Do you want more freedom? If so, ask a pheasant to show you how to become more independent and adventurous. A pheasant can also help you display your features and qualities advantageously, in order to impress others. When you need to apply yourself in a practical and productive way, let a pheasant guide you.

Symbolic meanings: A pheasant may appear to you in real life or a dream when you feel restricted by responsibilities or rules. It might encourage you to find ways to enjoy more freedom. A pheasant could also recommend using your talents and ideas in a more practical manner.

Phoenix

Characteristics: The mythical phoenix symbolizes the cycle of birth, death, and rebirth. Like the phoenix, you have probably experienced many ups and downs in your lifetime. Even though you may have endured hardship and loss, you've managed to transcend the difficulties and come out a better person. You have amazing powers of renewal and rejuvenation. You're a survivor, and know how to rise above suffering instead of letting it break your spirit. Most likely, the trials and tribulations you've undergone have heightened your spiritual awareness.

Strengths: Resilience, spiritual awareness, faith

Weaknesses: Physical illnesses

How to use this creature's power: When you are going through a difficult time, ask a phoenix to guide you and help you come out stronger. If you're suffering with an illness or injury, a phoenix can aid your recovery. A phoenix can teach you how to maintain faith even during the darkest moments.

Symbolic meanings: If you see a phoenix in a dream or vision, it means that you are now or soon will be going through a transition. Something in your life is dying so that something else can emerge. A phoenix may tell you to rise above a difficult situation and trust that things will get better.

Pigeon

Characteristics: Like the pigeon, which can always find its way home, you feel a strong attachment to your home and family. Although you may travel far and wide, you always return to your roots. You also know how to "home in" on what you want in life and pursue it with clarity. Because pigeons carried messages before the days of modern communication, you are probably adept at communicating and may work in a field that uses this skill.

Strengths: Sense of direction, communication skills, appreciation of your heritage

Weaknesses: Tendency to cling to the past

How to use this bird's power: If you're feeling insecure, a pigeon can show you how to reconnect with your sense of inner stability. If you need direction, let a pigeon show you the way. When you travel, invite a pigeon to accompany you—you won't get lost. If you're having trouble getting your message across, a pigeon can serve as your go-between.

Symbolic meanings: If you see a pigeon in the physical world or a dream, it may advise you to reconnect with who you are at a fundamental level. A pigeon might appear when you feel homesick and long for your home and family. Sometimes it shows up to warn you that you may be a "pigeon" and get blamed for someone else's mistakes.

Puffin

Characteristics: Imaginative and intuitive, you have the ability to express yourself in a creative way, perhaps as an artist, musician, or poet. You dive deep into the mysterious realms of your psyche to bring forth inspiration. However, your inconsistency and impracticality can make it hard for you to bring your vision down to earth. You can be quite sociable and affectionate, but if someone "ruffles your feathers," you turn cold instantly. It's important for you to stay balanced emotionally and not behave like a drama queen. Try not to see things as simply black or white, but exquisitely nuanced.

Strengths: Imagination, intuition, artistic ability, sensitivity

Weaknesses: Impracticality, temperamental nature, emotional imbalance, idealism

How to use this bird's power: A puffin can help you sense emotional undercurrents and ride them gracefully. It can also help you reach deep into your subconscious to discover the treasures that lie within.

Symbolic meanings: The presence of a puffin in real life or a dream might warn you to be careful about the messages you send to others, nonverbally as well as verbally. Be honest with others and yourself. A puffin's appearance may coincide with an emotional period, and encourage you to draw creative inspiration from the experience.

Quail

Characteristics: If this small game bird is your totem, you exhibit a strong appreciation for your community, like the quail does. You enjoy participating in groups and understand the value of teamwork. An excellent networker, you know how to combine your resources with other people's so that everyone benefits. You can bring people together to support a worthy cause, to collaborate on a project, or to have a good time. Always alert to things that could endanger the safety and well-being of your community, you might choose a career in police work or social services.

Strengths: Sociability, networking ability, awareness

Weaknesses: Hypervigilance, nervousness, dependence on others

How to use this bird's power: Native American legend says a quail can help you discover your soul name and choose the right name for your new baby. A quail can show you how to handle group endeavors or expand your social network.

Symbolic meanings: If a quail appears to you, whether you're asleep or awake, it may warn you not to try something alone—there's safety in numbers. Perhaps you need to be more sociable. A quail might also recommend that you seek the support, protection, and nurturing of a group. Sometimes a quail's appearance warns you to be more alert to what's going on around you.

Roadrunner

Characteristics: Like your totem, you're blessed with swiftness and agility, both physically and mentally. Your brain is always running in high gear, and you know how to think on your feet. Not only are you full of ideas, you have a knack for putting them into action. If one plan doesn't work out, you deftly shift to another. You may have trouble collaborating, however, because most people simply can't keep up with you. Fortunately, you're inventive and self-motivated; you don't need anyone else to support or inspire you.

Strengths: Intelligence, speed, hardiness, agility, independence

Weaknesses: Mental stress, overstimulation, inconsistency

How to use this bird's power: When you need to think and act quickly, ask a roadrunner for guidance. A roadrunner can show you how to put your ideas into action or jumpstart a project. Do you have a tight deadline to meet? Call upon a roadrunner to lend you its speed.

Symbolic meanings: If you see a roadrunner in the waking world or a dream, it may tell you either to stop stalling and get busy, or, conversely, to slow down and stop rushing around. A roadrunner might also appear when you need to change direction quickly and take another path.

Robin

Characteristics: The first birds to show up in the springtime, robins represent new beginnings. If the robin is your totem, you probably have an adventurous spirit and are the first one to try something new. You're not easily daunted by difficult situations, and enjoy a challenge. You may also be an avatar or visionary who alerts others to what lies ahead. Never afraid to speak your mind, you like to debate and can be a bit argumentative. Perhaps your strong communication skills can benefit you professionally. Many robin people like music and enjoy singing.

Strengths: Adventurousness, hardiness, verbal skill, musical talent

Weaknesses: Argumentativeness, recklessness

How to use this bird's power: Do you want to be more daring or break out of a rut? Call upon a robin to show you how to do it with style. Ask a robin to help you speak up and express your ideas without fear of ridicule. A robin can also assist you in developing your musical talent.

Symbolic meanings: If you see a robin in real life or a dream, remember the saying "the early bird gets the worm"—you might need to try harder or be more alert in order to get the jump on the competition. A robin's appearance could foretell a new beginning or advise you to try something new.

Rooster

Characteristics: The rooster ushers in the dawn with its raucous crow, and like it, you may be the avatar who alerts others to what's on the horizon. You sense when something new is about to break and can often be found in the vanguard of movements, ventures, or discoveries. Because one rooster can service scores of hens, this totem is also associated with fertility. You, too, might be quite creative and fertile, either physically or mentally. However, you may also think highly of yourself and "crow" about your abilities or accomplishments.

Strengths: Forward thinking, alertness, creativity, protectiveness

Weaknesses: Lack of direction, arrogance, argumentativeness

How to use this bird's power: A rooster can point out what's imminent, so that you're ready when a new trend or opportunity dawns. It can also teach you how to wake up your creativity and be more productive. If you tend to be too modest, a rooster can show you how to promote yourself and your ideas.

Symbolic meanings: If you see a rooster in the waking world or a dream, it's usually a wake-up call; pay attention. A rooster's appearance can herald an upcoming event or experience. Sometimes this barnyard bird shows up to advise you not to be "cocky."

Sandpiper

Characteristics: Witty and cheerful, you don't take life too seriously and can help other people to lighten up as well. Even during emotionally challenging periods, you stay grounded; when the waters get too turbulent, you know when to retreat to dry land. Always busy, you have a variety of interests and activities, and constantly explore new ideas. In following your curiosity, however, you may poke your nose into a number of things briefly, then lose interest and dart off to something else. You may love haunting flea markets and yard sales, and usually find treasures hidden among the trash.

Strengths: Cheerfulness, curiosity, versatility, resourcefulness

Weaknesses: Indecision, inconsistency, superficiality

How to use this bird's power: When you're trying to decide what you want to do with your life, ask a sandpiper to explore different options with you. Take a sandpiper with you on a shopping trip—it can show you how to get the best deals. If you're in the throes of an emotional situation, a sandpiper can help you ride the waves and find your way safely back to shore.

Symbolic meanings: If you see a sandpiper in real life or a dream, it may advise you to scavenge something of value from an unpleasant experience or situation. It might also recommend "testing the waters" and exploring a number of possibilities before making a decision.

Snow (Blue) Goose

Characteristics: People who have the wild snow goose as a totem display many of the same qualities as domesticated goose people. However, you're more freedom loving and not so attached to your property. You also like to travel—preferably with friends, family, or a group—and may take frequent trips or relocate regularly. When a situation requires it, you can change your colors in order to adapt. Ambitious and intelligent, you aim for the sky and have the ability to soar to great heights. You might even be a visionary of sorts who can see into the future.

Strengths: Intelligence, vision, versatility, sociability

Weaknesses: Perfectionism, instability, vociferousness

How to use this bird's power: If you feel stuck in a rut, ask a snow goose to help you make a change that will give you more freedom or success. If you're going on a trip, invite a snow goose to accompany and protect you. This bird can also help you learn new subjects or communicate more effectively.

Symbolic meanings: When a snow goose shows up, in the waking world or in a dream, it can mean you're about to go on a trip. Sometimes this bird's appearance advises you to make a change or to give up an attachment. It might also warn you to keep your eyes open; to be on the lookout either for opportunities or danger.

Sparrow

Characteristics: Traditionally, the sparrow represented the common classes in Europe. If this is your totem, you are content to live a simple life without ostentation. You don't feel a need to impress others or to be special; you understand what's really important, and are more interested in spiritual abundance than material wealth. Prolific and resilient, you know how to survive and thrive despite hardships. You hold your own when challenged, even against powerful opponents, without losing your dignity.

Strengths: Self-reliance, confidence, modesty, resiliency

Weaknesses: Lack of ambition or imagination

How to use this bird's power: A sparrow can show you how to maintain your dignity during difficult times. If you feel insecure or inadequate, a sparrow can teach you self-worth. Is someone trying to overpower or take advantage of you? Ask a sparrow to help you take back what's yours.

Symbolic meanings: If you see a sparrow in real life or a dream, it may remind you to value yourself and recognize your inherent worth, regardless of your position in society. If you've been "trying to keep up with the Joneses," a sparrow might advise you to live more simply or to be content with what you have and who you are.

Starling

Characteristics: Like this bird, you're very sociable and probably have an extensive network of friends and acquaintances. You might belong to a number of social and professional groups and understand the importance of teamwork. With your ability to bring people together to get a job done, you could excel in any career that involves organizing others. You appreciate society's rules of conduct and function smoothly within your community. However, you tend to be a follower rather than a leader. You go along to get along, and might allow other people to think for you.

Strengths: Sociability, sense of etiquette, community spirit

Weaknesses: Dependence on others, lack of originality, mob/gang behavior

How to use this bird's power: A starling can teach you how to operate effectively within a group. It can help you understand what's expected of you and how to behave in a particular circumstance. This bird can also help you gain acceptance into a group you want to join. If you're shy or have trouble getting along with other people, ask a starling to show you how to be more sociable.

Symbolic meanings: If you see a starling in its natural habitat or a dream, it could mean you're losing yourself in the crowd. A starling might suggest you need to adjust your behavior in order to get along better with other people.

Stork

Characteristics: In folklore, storks are said to bring babies, and if this is your totem you might choose a career as a pediatrician or midwife. You probably love children and enjoy caring for them. Protective and nurturing, you create a comfortable home for your loved ones, and your family is very important to you. The stork wades in water and captures fish with its long beak, which symbolizes your ability to connect with your emotions and use your intuition productively to nourish yourself and others.

Strengths: Protectiveness, nurturing nature, creativity, intuition, feminine power

Weaknesses: Oversensitivity, emotional imbalance

How to use this bird's power: If you want to have a baby, invite a stork into your life. A stork can also assist you in birthing a new project or venture. Do you want to rediscover the joy you knew as a child? Ask a stork to show you how.

Symbolic meanings: A stork seen either in the waking world or a dream could presage the birth of something new. It can also signal a change in your family situation. A stork's appearance might advise you to nurture yourself or someone else. Seeing a stork may also mean you need to reconnect with your roots or get in touch with your inner child.

Swallow

Characteristics: The graceful swallow spends much of its time in the air, which symbolizes your inclination to devote yourself mainly to intellectual and spiritual pursuits. A lifelong student, you probably have many interests and enjoy learning new things. You like sharing what you know with others, and your well-developed communication skills could make you a good teacher, writer, or orator. In your quest for knowledge, however, you may ignore the mundane aspects of living and have your head in the clouds.

Strengths: Intelligence, spirituality, communication skills

Weaknesses: Flightiness, impracticality, idealism

How to use this bird's power: A swallow can assist you in learning a new subject or skill. If you feel trapped by mundane matters or you've gotten into a rut, a swallow can teach you how to set your sights higher and soar. Ask a swallow to guide you in making a presentation, writing a paper, speaking in public, or communicating your ideas to others.

Symbolic meanings: If a swallow appears to you in the waking world or a dream, it may advise you to rise above petty annoyances and problems to move ahead with your life. Perhaps you need to see things from a new perspective. Sometimes a swallow encourages you to pay more attention to spiritual or intellectual concerns.

Swan

Characteristics: A symbol of love and beauty, the graceful swan mates for life. If this is your totem, relationships and romance are important to you. You love deeply, and once you make a commitment you remain faithful to your partner through good times and bad. Sensitive, intuitive, and emotional, you see the goodness in others and appreciate their inner beauty rather than focusing merely on external appearances. Your innate balance, grace, and imagination could enable you to excel at poetry, music, or another art form. The swan's lifespan equals that of humans, and, like it, you may enjoy a long, healthy life.

Strengths: Beauty, grace, loyalty, balance, imagination, longevity

Weaknesses: Idealism, oversensitivity

How to use this bird's power: If you're having trouble in a relationship, ask a swan to help you resolve difficulties. A swan can teach you the value of fidelity. It can also show you how to glide gracefully through emotional situations and stay balanced, instead of letting your feelings overwhelm you.

Symbolic meanings: If you see a swan in real life or a dream, it could mean love is in the air—a new romantic relationship may begin or an existing one might improve. A swan's appearance may encourage you to see your own or someone else's inner beauty.

Turkey

Characteristics: The turkey is associated with the harvest season, and if this is your totem you have a knack for creating abundance. You know how to bring your ideas down to earth and apply them in practical ways, so that you and others can reap rewards. Family- and community-oriented, you engage in cooperative activities that benefit the collective. You also accept assistance from others when needed. "Share and share alike" might be your motto. Like peacock people, you can show off at times, and men with this totem especially may be a bit vain.

Strengths: Cooperation, practicality, generosity, prosperity

Weaknesses: Cockiness, vanity

How to use this bird's power: A turkey can teach you how to cooperate with others and how to combine your resources for the good of all. Ask a turkey to help you "bring in the harvest" and prosper from your labors.

Symbolic meanings: If a turkey appears to you in real life or a dream, it could mean you're about to reap rewards. A turkey's appearance might also advise you to be more community-minded rather than selfish. Sometimes a turkey shows up when you need to present yourself in a more impressive way, or, conversely, when you're behaving in a cocky manner.

Vulture

Characteristics: Because vultures eat carrion, they're linked with death. If this is your totem, you may be intrigued by the cycle of birth, death, and rebirth, and the mysteries of the world beyond this one. Like the vulture, you're very resourceful; you know how to find what you need and make do with what you have. Perhaps you enjoy scavenging through flea markets and thrift stores to find treasures, and you're a proponent of conservation and recycling. Your keen senses enable you to home in on what you want—you might even possess ESP or see auras.

Strengths: Sensory awareness, resourcefulness, vision

Weaknesses: Messiness, indulgence, lack of discrimination

How to use this bird's power: A vulture can show you how to make the best of a bad situation and to find "silver linings." If you must perform an unpleasant task, the vulture can help you find meaning and purpose in what you do. Ask a vulture to teach you the mysteries of life and death.

Symbolic meanings: If you spot a vulture in real life or a dream, it might tell you to look more deeply into a matter or to view it from a different perspective. A vulture's appearance could warn you to be more discriminating and use your sharp senses to detect something rotten.

Waxwing

Characteristics: Courteous and considerate of others, you're skilled in social graces and know how to behave in all situations. Your pleasant demeanor and good manners make you a welcome guest and a delightful companion. However, you tend to be shy and don't reveal yourself right away. You realize that people can take advantage of your gentle and unassuming nature, and may use etiquette to keep emotional distance between you and others. The waxwing's markings include a mask on its face, and like your totem, you might hide your true nature behind a mask.

Strengths: Consideration, gentleness, good manners

Weaknesses: Secretiveness, vulnerability, timidity

How to use this bird's power: In social situations—especially ones where you feel awkward or out of place—ask a waxwing to show you how to behave properly. A waxwing can help you to be more considerate of others and give them the respect they deserve. If you want to present a certain image, a waxwing can teach you how to make the right impression.

Symbolic meanings: If you see a waxwing in real life or a dream, it may mean you aren't being courteous or considerate of someone else. Conversely, it might point out that others aren't showing you the respect you deserve. A waxwing could also fly into your life when you're hiding behind a mask, afraid to show your true self.

Woodpecker

Characteristics: You display great persistence and determination when it comes to digging deeply into situations. Not satisfied with superficialities, you probe beneath the surface to discover what lies within. You hold firmly to your position and don't back down until you've accomplished your goal. With your individualistic spirit, you usually rely on your own inner guidance and experience. You like to do things in your own unique way. Because this bird's rhythmic pecking sounds drum-like, some people with a woodpecker totem have natural rhythm and enjoy drumming.

Strengths: Determination, self-reliance, insight

Weaknesses: Stubbornness, repetitiveness

How to use this bird's power: Call upon a woodpecker to assist you with a project that requires patience and persistence. If you want to discover a secret or find something that's hidden, ask a woodpecker to be your guide. This bird can also help you be more independent and to follow your own path.

Symbolic meanings: A woodpecker could advise you to delve more deeply into a matter—don't just accept what's apparent. If you see one of these birds, whether outside or in a dream, it might also mean you need to be more diligent, or, conversely, that you need to break away from the repetitive pattern you're in.

Wren

Characteristics: You may not be large or physically powerful, but you don't back down from challenges, and can use your cleverness to best a stronger opponent. Your verbal ability enables you to talk your way into positions of advantage and out of dangerous spots. Known for your resourcefulness, you learn from others' mistakes. You're also adept at taking someone else's ideas and making them your own. Regardless of the position you were born into, you believe in yourself, and your confidence helps you to succeed.

Strengths: Adaptability, resourcefulness, self-confidence, verbal skills

Weaknesses: Arrogance, egotism

How to use this bird's power: If you don't feel capable of handling a task, ask a wren to show you how to maximize your abilities. This little bird can teach you how to value yourself more. It can also help you speak up for yourself.

Symbolic meanings: If a wren appears to you in real life or a dream, it might advise you to use your resources and other people's more effectively. A wren can also recommend going after what you want with more enthusiasm and confidence. Sometimes a wren appears when you need to be more flexible and adapt to the circumstances in which you find yourself.

"When we get discouraged, we could all learn a thing or two from insect animal totem meanings. It's their unsinkable nature that reminds us to keep moving forward for progress."

—Avia Venefica, *www.whats-your-sign.com*

Insects

Ant

Characteristics: Industrious, like the ant, you're willing to work hard to accomplish your objectives. You don't expect overnight results. By creating a firm foundation and building upon it in a careful, organized fashion, you achieve enduring success. People with this totem make good architects, carpenters, stonemasons, and other construction workers. Often you devote yourself to the good of the group, and combine your energy and skills with those of others toward a common goal. Perhaps you're a pillar in your community. You appreciate structure and order in all areas of life, and respect time-honored traditions.

Strengths: Industriousness, diligence, organization, community spirit

Weaknesses: Repetitiveness, rigidity, workaholism

How to use this insect's power: If you want to bring your dreams to fruition, an ant can teach you how to be more persistent. Ask an ant to assist you in building a business or laying the foundation for a new project. An ant can also help you create structure and order in your personal or professional life.

Symbolic meanings: If you see an ant in the physical world or a dream, it could mean you need to work harder to succeed at something. On the other hand, an ant's appearance might suggest you've been working too hard and need to take a break. Sometimes an ant advises working with others instead of going it alone.

Bee

Characteristics: You've heard the saying "busy as a bee," and if the bee is your spirit guide, you possess boundless energy and work tirelessly to achieve your goals. In addition to your regular job, you may have an avocation that you enjoy plus lots of activities you engage in, so you have little downtime. Your team spirit enables you to work well with others to increase your output, and you may be very good at making money or creating highly valued products. However, you can be a bit touchy, and when upset you attack with speed and accuracy.

Strengths: Industriousness, productivity, creativity, cooperation

Weaknesses: Excessive busyness, temperamental nature, quick to anger

How to use this insect's power: When you need creative inspiration or determination, ask a bee to assist you. A bee can show you how to skillfully build anything from a model car to a skyscraper. If you're under attack, a bee can be your ally and help you fight off your enemy.

Symbolic meanings: If you encounter a bee in real life or a dream, it could mean you're too busy and need to rest. Conversely, it might urge you to get busy and stop procrastinating.

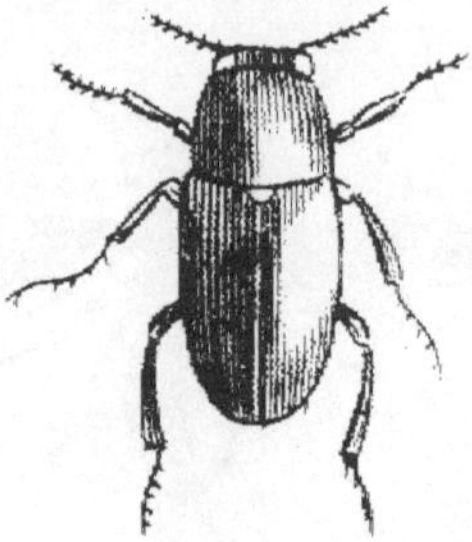

Beetle

Characteristics: The ancient Egyptians considered the scarab a symbol of the soul. Like most beetles, it transforms from a grub to an adult beetle during its life cycle, and you may experience many similar ups and downs in your lifetime. However, you persist through the changes without losing faith, allowing them to shape and teach you. Perhaps a belief in a higher power gives you strength and direction. You have the ability to protect yourself and to prosper even when the odds are against you. At times, though, your hard-shelled nature can prevent others from getting close to you.

Strengths: Endurance, adaptability, faith, spirituality

Weaknesses: Rigidity, overprotectiveness

How to use this insect's power: A beetle can guide you during a period of change and show you how to evolve through the experience. When you're faced with difficult challenges, a beetle can teach you how to protect yourself. Ask a beetle to guide you on a spiritual quest.

Symbolic meanings: If you see a beetle in nature or while you're dreaming, it could mean a change is in store. Or, it might suggest that you need to make a change and let go of the past. Sometimes a beetle shows up during a difficult time to let you know there's light at the end of the tunnel.

Butterfly

Characteristics: Although we admire the delicate beauty of butterflies, these amazing insects possess tremendous strength—some of them migrate thousands of miles each year. Like them, you blend grace with tenacity and are probably tougher than you appear. Carefree and curious, you want to experience everything life has to offer; as a result, you flit from one thing to another and may have trouble making commitments. You've probably experienced many changes during your lifetime and barely resemble the person you were years ago.

Strengths: Flexibility, beauty, cheerfulness, sociability

Weaknesses: Superficiality, fickleness

How to use this insect's power: Invite a butterfly to accompany you on a trip—you'll have more fun. Let a butterfly help you meet new people or become more popular. Butterfly power can help you deal with life's ups and downs, and handle challenges with grace and optimism.

Symbolic meanings: When a butterfly shows up in waking life or in a dream, it's a sign that a change is coming. If you're in the midst of a transformation, a butterfly encourages you to lighten up and embrace the change. Butterflies also urge you to emerge from your cocoon and show off your true beauty.

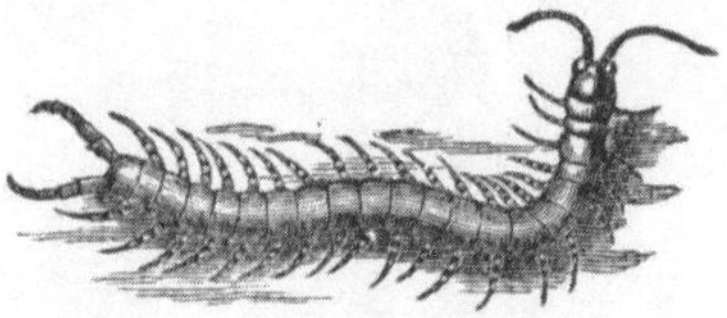

Centipede

Characteristics: Legs allow you to move about in the world, and if the centipede (or millipede) is your totem you travel through life with ease and grace. Physically coordinated and dexterous, you might possess athletic ability or enjoy dancing. You also know how to use your many talents harmoniously to facilitate progress in all areas of your life. Like your totem, which grows more legs as it matures, you might be a "late bloomer." Security is important to you, and your ability to stay grounded can help you to get where you want to go. However, you don't like being in the spotlight and may be shy or antisocial.

Strengths: Balance, coordination, stability

Weaknesses: Reclusiveness, difficulties in early life

How to use this insect's power: A centipede can help you become more coordinated, and if you want to dance or run better, ask this insect to assist you. If you tend to be flaky, let a centipede teach you how to become more grounded.

Symbolic meanings: If you see a centipede in real life or a dream, it could recommend finding balance and harmony in some area. Perhaps you need to coordinate your efforts better in order to accomplish an objective. A centipede might show up to warn you to "crawl under a rock" and not draw attention to yourself.

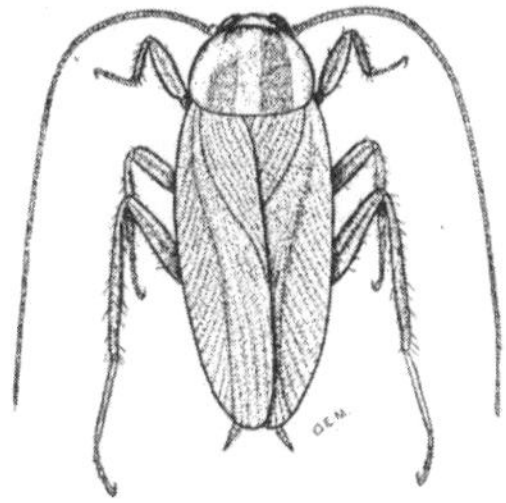

Cockroach

Characteristics: Resourceful and tenacious, you don't give up easily and can find within yourself whatever you need to get along. You possess strong survival skills and can adapt to conditions that would destroy other less hardy individuals. If faced with a hostile situation, you know how to scurry away to safer ground. Not very sociable, you usually prefer a quiet, reclusive life and stay out of sight as much as possible. Because cockroaches are one of the oldest species on the planet, people with this totem may enjoy long, healthy lives.

Strengths: Resourcefulness, adaptability, good survival skills, self-reliance, longevity

Weaknesses: Reclusiveness, antisocial behavior, fearfulness

How to use this insect's power: If you find yourself in a difficult position, ask a cockroach to lend you its survival skills. A roach can also teach you how to adapt to changing environments or conditions. Call on a roach to help you develop your personal resources and become more self-reliant.

Symbolic meanings: If you encounter a cockroach in the here and now or while dreaming, it might mean you need to clean up some area of your life. It might also warn you to get out of the way of danger—run and hide. Sometimes a roach shows up to advise you to spend more time alone, instead of socializing so much.

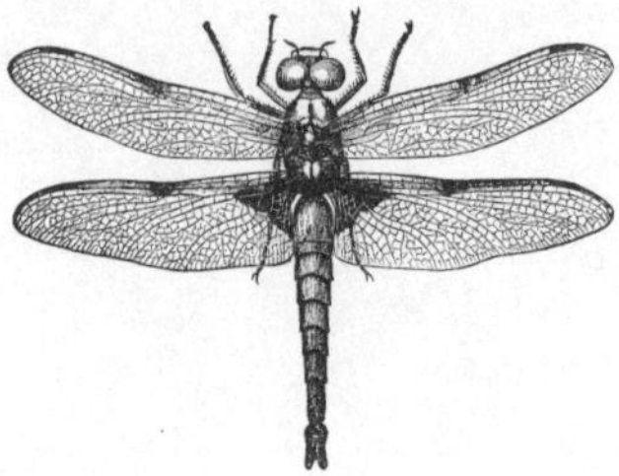

Dragonfly/Damselfly

Characteristics: Because dragonflies are at home in both the air and water, people with this totem display both intellectual and emotional power. However, you might have trouble balancing these two parts of your personality. Your behavior can also be unpredictable or erratic, especially during your youth. Like your totem, you "change colors" depending on conditions, and you may seem different to different people or in different circumstances. You enjoy being in the spotlight, and with your dazzling presence you could succeed as an actor, musician, or other performer.

Strengths: Beauty, colorful personality, versatility

Weaknesses: Inconsistency, emotional imbalance

How to use this insect's power: When you want to make a showy appearance or create an illusion, ask a dragonfly to teach you its beauty secrets. A dragonfly can also help you draw upon both your intellect and intuition to achieve your objectives. If you've shut down emotionally and want to experience more passion in life, invite a dragonfly to guide you.

Symbolic meanings: A dragonfly's appearance might encourage you to reflect light and joy from higher sources into the world around you. It could also advise you to balance your mind and emotions.

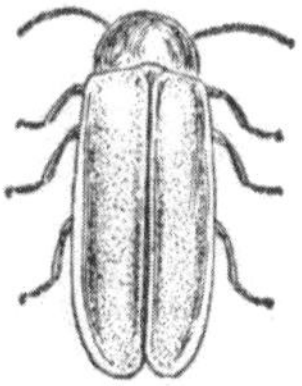

Firefly/Lightning Bug

Characteristics: Like your totem, you shine light into dark situations. By holding a lantern for other people, you help them to see more clearly. Your sparkling nature can also inspire others to find their own "light," and perhaps to discover the spiritual gifts that lie within. You focus on the joys in life instead of wasting energy wallowing in negativity; you know that your thoughts and feelings create your reality. Even under difficult conditions, you remain optimistic and infuse hope into all you do. Like the firefly, you're probably a night person and glow more brightly after dark.

Strengths: Optimism, cheerfulness, clarity, inspiration

Weaknesses: Idealism, flightiness

How to use this insect's power: During a difficult time, when all seems dark and desolate, ask a firefly to bring you hope. Are you wasting energy worrying about something? A firefly can teach you how to use your vitality and talents more efficiently.

Symbolic meanings: If you see a firefly while awake or in a dream, it might encourage you to lighten up and be more positive. Focus on the light at the end of the tunnel, instead of the momentary darkness. When a firefly flashes, it may signal you to look carefully at something.

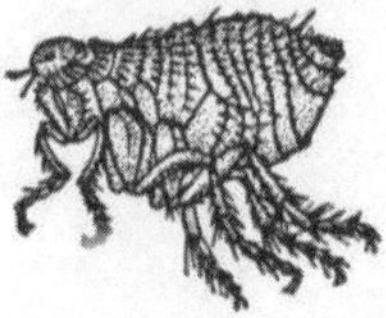

Flea

Characteristics: Like the flea, you quickly leap at opportunities and sink your teeth into them, thereby getting the jump on competitors. Your speed and dexterity also enable you to hop out of the way of danger. Resilient, resourceful, and self-reliant, you know how to get the most out of whatever comes your way. You're also much hardier than you appear, and can survive even in difficult situations. Once you undertake something, you cling tenaciously to your goal and can succeed through sheer willpower.

Strengths: Resourcefulness, determination, hardiness, self-sufficiency

Weaknesses: Opportunism, ruthlessness, stubbornness, tendency to annoy others

How to use this insect's power: If you feel powerless or threatened, a flea can help you recognize that you are stronger and more resilient than you think. A flea can also show you how to jump at opportunities and take advantage of situations.

Symbolic meanings: If you see a flea in real life or a dream, it could mean an irritation is gnawing at you. Perhaps you feel someone or something is sucking your "blood" (vitality). A flea might also encourage you to get more out of life: sink your teeth into something you feel passionate about and let it nourish you.

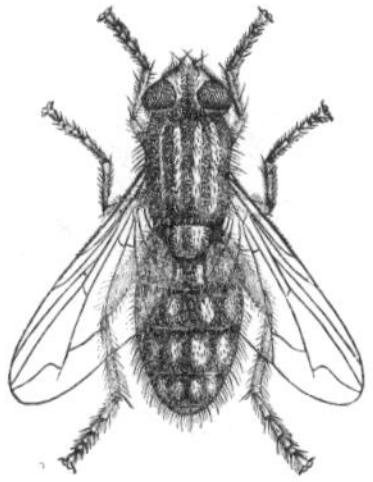

Fly

Characteristics: With your acute vision, you can view life from many perspectives in order to understand people and situations clearly. Your heightened awareness allows you to thrive even in unfavorable circumstances. When danger threatens, you fly out of the way unscathed. You know how to use your assets wisely and see value in things other people consider worthless. As a result, you can transform trash into treasure.

Strengths: Vision, sensory awareness, resourcefulness, ability to thrive in difficult conditions

Weaknesses: Uncleanliness, lack of discrimination

How to use this insect's power: A fly can teach you how to see something in many different ways and come to a new appreciation of it. When you need to get out of harm's way, let this insect show you how to fly away. If you feel life has dealt you a bad hand, ask a fly to help you extract value from the dregs.

Symbolic meanings: If you see a fly in real life or encounter it in a dream, it may mean you're turning small annoyances into big ones. Perhaps you need to take a broader view of something, in order to ascertain its significance. Sometimes spotting a fly can be a play on words, predicting a plane trip.

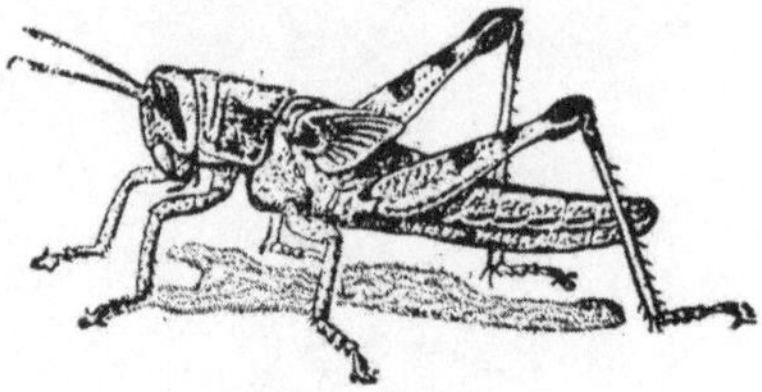

Grasshopper

Characteristics: If the grasshopper is your totem, you progress through life by leaps and bounds, just as this insect takes great leaps forward. You quickly jump at chances that come your way and might succeed in unexpected areas. However, you don't move in a straight line and can end up way off course at times. Trusting your own instincts and your unique way of doing things will enable you to achieve more than you could by following other people's dictates.

Strengths: Ingenuity, uniqueness, individuality

Weaknesses: Lack of direction, instability

How to use this insect's power: Ask a grasshopper to help you take a leap of faith into uncharted territory. It can show you how to approach a matter in an unusual or indirect way, when going at it head on hasn't worked. A grasshopper can also teach you how to become comfortable with your own rhythms and style.

Symbolic meanings: If you encounter a grasshopper in its natural habitat or while dreaming, it may advise you to jump at—or away from—something. A grasshopper may appear when your personal or professional life is about to take a leap forward. Sometimes seeing a grasshopper indicates that you've gotten off track and are in danger of losing your way.

Ladybug

Characteristics: Like other beetles and butterflies, ladybugs metamorphose from eggs to grubs to flying insects; consequently, people with this totem often experience many transformations in life. You may find that, as an adult, you feel little connection with your childhood. Perhaps you'll change careers or locales many times, or you may simply like making changes in your home or personal appearance. Ladybugs are symbols of good luck, and you might consider yourself more fortunate than most people. With your colorful personality and attractiveness, you are probably quite popular. You may love the sun and feel more comfortable in warm climates.

Strengths: Sunny personality, luckiness, practicality

Weaknesses: Inconsistency, flightiness, oversensitivity to environmental factors

How to use this insect's power: If you are in the midst of an upsetting change, a ladybug can guide you through the challenges to better times ahead. If you feel stuck or bored, ask a ladybug to help you try something new and different. Call upon a ladybug when you need some good luck.

Symbolic meanings: Seeing a ladybug flying about or encountering one in a dream can alert you to a change in the future. Often the change is a fortunate one. A ladybug might also encourage you to make a change that will bring you more happiness.

Locust

Characteristics: Similar to people with the grasshopper totem, you quickly leap at opportunities that come your way. Often you succeed at ventures because you are willing to take the road less traveled or to pursue a matter in an unconventional way. Once you start something, you don't look back. However, your ambition can get out of hand at times and you may take advantage of others or move ruthlessly into someone else's territory. Like the locust, you have exceptional communication skills and perhaps a strong singing voice; singing in a chorus might appeal to you.

Strengths: Good communication skills, optimism, singing ability

Weaknesses: Destructiveness, boastfulness, raucousness, greed

How to use this insect's power: When you need to get the jump on others, ask a locust to help you move quickly and seize the advantage. A locust can also show you how to change directions and try something new or different.

Symbolic meanings: If you run across a locust in real life or in a dream, it could advise you to leap ahead and take a chance. This insect might also appear when you're being greedy. Sometimes a locust shows up to warn you that someone is about to take advantage of you and destroy what you've created.

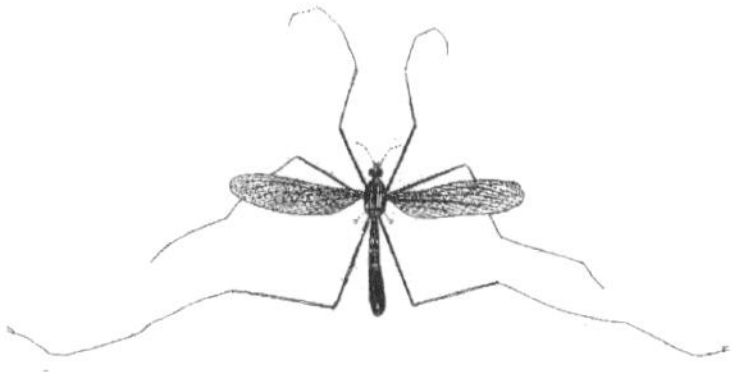

Mosquito

Characteristics: The female mosquito draws blood from other creatures to nourish and protect her young. If this is your totem, you possess strong nurturing and protective traits and are probably a devoted parent. You also know how to use the energy available to you in your environment and make the most of what life has to offer you. Your keen awareness enables you to detect opportunities and home in on them. One of your talents is your ability to use other people's energy and resources to your advantage. Because only the female mosquito bites, this can be the totem of dynamic women.

Strengths: Feminine power, nurturing qualities, protectiveness, vitality

Weaknesses: Parasitic behavior, tendency to irritate other people

How to use this insect's power: Does your life lack excitement and joy? If so, ask a mosquito to show you how to bite into what you want and to draw more juice from your experiences. A mosquito can help you get in touch with feminine power and passion. It can also teach you how to nurture yourself and others.

Symbolic meanings: If you see a mosquito in nature or dream of one, it could mean something in waking life is biting at you—examine your environment to determine what's causing an irritation. Is someone or something draining your vitality? Perhaps you need to protect yourself from attack or set better boundaries.

Praying Mantis

Characteristics: A spiritual path is important to people with this totem, and you may engage in prayer or meditation regularly. In order to stay balanced, you need periods of quiet. This allows you to receive wisdom from higher sources and to hear the still, small voice within. When faced with a problem, you can find the answer in yourself. You also know how to withdraw from people or situations that drain your energy and focus on what's beneficial to you. Perhaps you find martial arts, which combine quiet contemplation with action, appealing.

Strengths: Spirituality, balance, stillness, inner wisdom

Weaknesses: Tendency to isolate yourself from others

How to use this insect's power: If you're wasting energy on things that aren't good for you, a praying mantis can show you how to be more discriminating. It can also teach you how to meditate to improve your concentration, reduce stress, and heal yourself in body, mind, and spirit.

Symbolic meanings: If you see a praying mantis in waking life or in a dream, it might advise you to be still and conserve your energy. It could also encourage you to shift your focus from material to spiritual things. A praying mantis might show up to warn you to be quiet—don't reveal your intentions at this time.

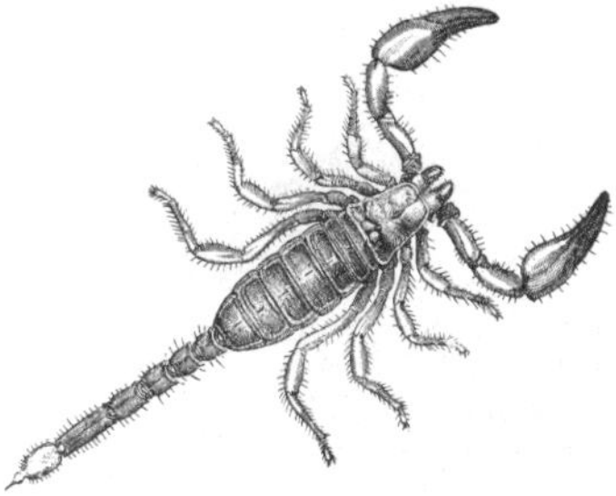

Scorpion

Characteristics: If this is your totem you've likely experienced many ups and downs during your lifetime. You understand the mysteries of life and death, perhaps through personal experience. To avoid the pain of loss, you've developed strong defenses. If you feel threatened, you attack with speed and accuracy. However, you tend toward skepticism and may see danger where none exists. Passionate and highly sexual, you easily attract partners, but your relationships can be tumultuous and you might need to learn to deal with a jealous streak.

Strengths: Resilience, inner strength, sex appeal, good defenses

Weaknesses: Skepticism, aggressiveness, jealousy, vindictiveness

How to use this insect's power: If you long for a passionate love affair, ask a scorpion to help you dazzle a partner—but be careful what you ask for! A scorpion can guide you through a difficult transformation or the literal or figurative death of something. It can also teach you how to defend yourself against attack.

Symbolic meanings: If you encounter a scorpion in real life or a dream, it may alert you to pending danger—defend yourself. Often it means a change is imminent. A scorpion's appearance might also coincide with a time of sexual passion, or advise you to control your passionate nature.

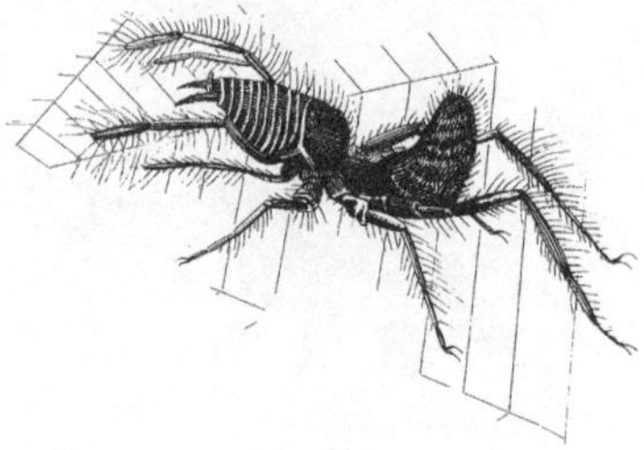

Spider

Characteristics: Industrious and imaginative, you work hard to bring your ideas to fruition. You like to see your creativity take physical form, and might excel at weaving, woodworking, interior design, or architecture. You skillfully use your talents to provide for yourself, just as the spider builds a web to capture its prey. In numerology, the spider's eight legs signify business acumen and material success. With your thoughts, emotions, and actions you weave your world into being, but you may need to learn how to trap what you want without trapping yourself in unhealthy, poisonous patterns.

Strengths: Creativity, industriousness, cleverness, feminine power

Weaknesses: Repetitiveness, slyness, deception

How to use this insect's power: A spider can show you how to use your creativity in a productive way, and how to weave your ideas into something useful. It can also teach you how to use subtlety and stealth to capture what you want.

Symbolic meanings: If you see a spider in nature or dream about one, it may presage a period of creative activity. A spider's appearance can warn you not to get caught in a web, either of your own making or someone else's. Sometimes a spider shows up to point out poisonous attitudes or behaviors.

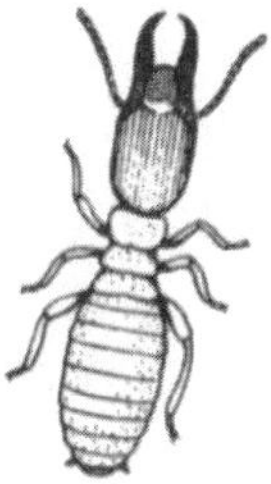

Termite

Characteristics: Like your totem, you're a tireless worker and energetically "bite through" obstacles in order to achieve your aims. Your determination and assertiveness enable you to accomplish a great deal in a short amount of time. Community-minded and cooperative, you can teach other people how to make the most of their talents. You function best when you can combine your abilities with those of others and work toward a common goal. A voracious seeker, you burrow deep into subjects that interest you and devour information at an astounding rate. You may have a tendency to overeat, and might need to watch your diet carefully.

Strengths: Determination, industriousness, cooperation

Weaknesses: Workaholism, eating disorders, destructiveness

How to use this insect's power: When you need to accomplish a lot in a short period of time, ask a termite to lend you its energy. A termite can also help you persevere through hardships, in order to accomplish your goals.

Symbolic meanings: If you see a termite in real life or a dream, it may warn you that someone or something is undermining your foundations. Perhaps your own attitudes or behaviors are destroying your stability. Sometimes a termite's appearance advises you to pay attention to your diet and to be more discriminating about what you eat.

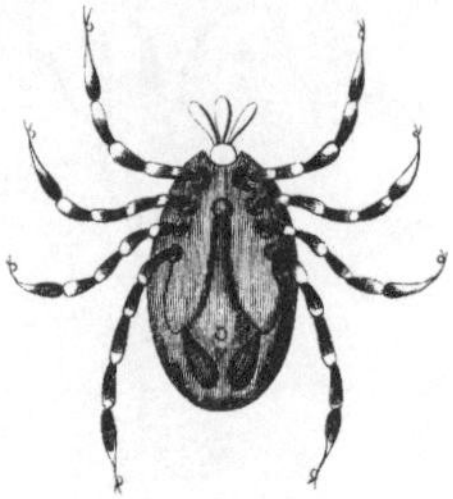

Tick

Characteristics: Unobtrusive and persistent, you know how to keep a low profile and not attract attention until you reach your goal. Your tough exterior enables you to protect yourself, even in hostile situations. Once you latch onto something, you hold on with tenacity and don't give up without a struggle. Because of your rigid nature and intransigence, however, you can get bogged down in routine. Your determination can help you "take a big bite" out of life and extract benefits from whatever you put your mind to, though your success may come at the expense of others.

Strengths: Tenacity, self-preservation skills

Weaknesses: Parasitic behavior, greed, stubbornness

How to use this insect's power: A tick can show you how to be more persistent in pursuing what you desire, especially if you think the goal is too big or out of your reach. It can also teach you how to hold on when the going gets tough.

Symbolic meanings: If you see a tick in waking life or a dream, it can warn that something or someone is sucking the life out of you. Conversely, it might mean you're taking advantage of someone else. Sometimes a tick's appearance encourages you to bite into something and hold on until you've drunk your fill.

Wasp/Hornet

Characteristics: You enjoy building things from the ground up. Whether your project is a house or a business, you apply your skills diligently and use available resources wisely to bring the task to fruition. You could succeed as an architect, carpenter, or entrepreneur. Good at working with other people, you can organize a group or team to get a job done faster. You aggressively pursue your goals and don't let anyone get in your way. If someone crosses you, however, you might behave vindictively, and you tend to hold on to grievances.

Strengths: Resourcefulness, constructiveness, determination, organizational skills

Weaknesses: Anger, spite, aggressiveness

How to use this insect's power: If you want to build a new home or a business, let a wasp assist you. When you need direction or determination, ask a wasp to guide you. A wasp can also teach you how to defend your territory.

Symbolic meanings: A wasp, whether seen or dreamed, could advise you to release anger or resentment, in order to establish a more peaceful relationship with someone. It might also suggest that you need to communicate better, without sarcasm or bitterness. Sometimes a wasp encourages you to pursue a course more directly or aggressively.

"The phenomenon of reptile body temperature changing with their surroundings makes them a supreme symbol of adaptation. As most reptiles' body functions depend on their body temperature this makes them dependent upon their surroundings too. Even so, reptiles are never slaves to external conditions. This is because they are super-intuitive, and fiercely independent."

—Avia Venefica, *www.whats-your-sign.com*

Reptiles and Amphibians

Alligator/Crocodile

Characteristics: Amazingly strong, quick, and ferocious, you attack life with gusto and fearlessly go after what you desire. However, you often conceal your intentions from others until the last moment, then swiftly seize your unsuspecting "quarry." This combination of strength and stealth make you a formidable opponent and fierce competitor. At times, you can be thick-skinned and inconsiderate of others. You're able to draw upon both physical and emotional power, and use your intuition as well as your physical abilities to make your way through life. Because alligators and crocodiles have lived on earth for millions of years, mythology links this totem with ancient wisdom.

Strengths: Physical power, fearlessness, speed, wisdom

Weaknesses: Aggressiveness, ruthlessness, cruelty

How to use this reptile's power: If you feel timid or weak, ask an alligator to lend you its great strength and ferociousness. Call upon an alligator whenever you need to act aggressively and decisively. An alligator can show you how to bide your time until just the right moment, then snag your prize.

Symbolic meanings: If you see an alligator or crocodile in the wild or a dream, it might advise you to bite through obstacles and seize the day. Sometimes it advises you to watch and wait for the right time to act. This reptile's appearance can also suggest that you're behaving in an insensitive or ruthless manner.

Chameleon

Characteristics: Your sensitivity to your surroundings and your keen awareness of what's required of you enable you to adapt to any situation with grace and ease. You use your astuteness, good manners, and social skills to fit into groups or environments, and could be an excellent diplomat. Quickly sizing up people and conditions is one of your specialties. However, your desire to please other people and be accepted can cause you to compromise your integrity or let others influence you too much.

Strengths: Adaptability, intuition, sensitivity to others

Weaknesses: Inconsistency, insincerity

How to use this reptile's power: If you need to adapt to changing circumstances, ask a chameleon to share its secrets with you. A chameleon can also teach you how to get along with people in diverse environments, and to understand the norms of a society or group.

Symbolic meanings: A chameleon seen in nature or your dreams might advise you to adapt to circumstances—change yourself instead of trying to change what's outside you. A chameleon's appearance could also encourage you to trust your perceptions and intuition. Sometimes a chameleon warns you not to blend into the crowd or let others set standards for you, or, conversely, that you need to be less conspicuous.

Dinosaur

Characteristics: With a dinosaur as your totem, you seek the wisdom of the ages and study the past to find out how to get along today. You learn from your mistakes and from the experiences of others. Perhaps you're a history buff or interested in mythology. A career in anthropology or archaeology might appeal to you. However, your focus on the past might prevent you from moving forward at today's rapid pace. Some of your ideas or behaviors may be out of date, and you can have trouble adapting to changes. Studying the individual characteristics of the different dinosaur species can help you understand your totem and yourself better.

Strengths: Ancient wisdom, appreciation of history

Weaknesses: Out of touch with the times, stubbornness

How to use this reptile's power: A dinosaur can help you see what you did wrong in a previous situation so that you don't make the same mistake again. If you're studying history, ask a dinosaur to take you on a journey back in time.

Symbolic meanings: If you encounter a dinosaur in a dream, a television program, or some other medium, it might mean you're stuck in the past and need to focus more on the present or future. A dinosaur can point out that if you don't change, you risk becoming "extinct" or passé. The type of dinosaur you see will give you additional information: a T. rex might advise you to be more aggressive or fearless, an Apatosaurus could remind you to eat your veggies.

Dragon

Characteristics: The Chinese consider the dragon a symbol of good luck, and like your totem, fortune may follow you wherever you go. Your dynamic presence strikes awe in the hearts of all who meet you, and you can seem a bit intimidating. Strong, wise, and physically impressive, you can easily rise to a position of power. A deep connection to the spiritual world enables you to tap into hidden wisdom and make use of it. As a result, you could become a powerful spiritual leader who inspires and guides others.

Strengths: Majestic appearance, strength, good luck, wisdom, spirituality

Weaknesses: Arrogance, fierceness, impracticality

How to use this creature's power: Call upon a dragon when you need extra strength or want to make an unforgettable impression: a dragon can show you how to amaze or intimidate other people. A dragon can bring good luck and inspiration in any endeavor. It can also guide you through a life transition, and connect you with your higher purpose.

Symbolic meanings: A dragon, whether encountered in a dream or other vision, can advise you to focus on your spiritual path as well as your material one. Perhaps you need to transcend mundane matters that are weighing you down. A dragon's appearance may alert you to a major change in the near future, perhaps a lucky one.

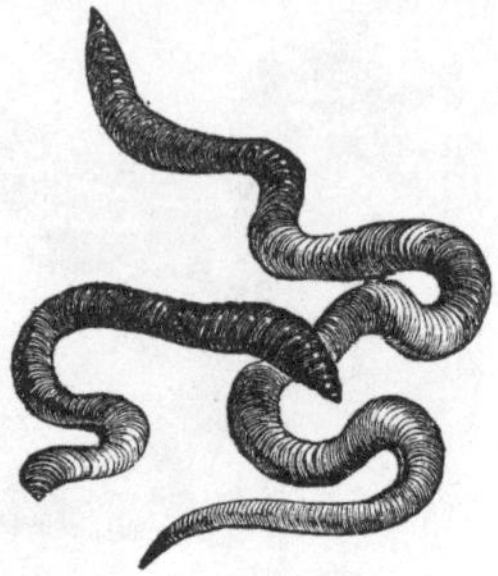

Earthworm

Characteristics: Superficial matters don't interest you; you burrow deep beneath the surface to nourish yourself with things of substance. You inch your way along slowly and carefully instead of acting in haste; as a result, you make steady, lasting progress. You aren't flashy and usually stay in the background, but your efforts can have an important impact. A tireless caretaker, you may devote yourself to helping others or saving the planet. Perhaps you love gardening and feel a strong connection with the earth.

Strengths: Persistence, depth of character, attention to detail, modesty

Weaknesses: Vulnerability, reclusiveness, lack of ambition

How to use this creature's power: When you need to work through a past issue and find meaning in it, ask an earthworm to guide you. If you usually rush into situations, an earthworm can show you how to approach a matter more slowly and carefully. If you're in the role of caretaker, an earthworm can teach you patience and acceptance.

Symbolic meanings: If you see an earthworm in nature or a dream, it might encourage you to dig more deeply into a subject or situation. An earthworm may appear when you need to digest an experience and decide what to keep from it and what to release. It might also warn you that someone is trying to "worm his way" into your life—don't leave yourself vulnerable.

Frog

Characteristics: Like your totem, you leap over problems and deftly jump out of the way when danger threatens. You've probably gone through many ups and downs during your lifetime, and have learned to adapt to changes. Sensitive and intuitive, you can read people and circumstances easily. Your deep emotions enable you to empathize with others, and you may choose a career in psychotherapy or the healing fields. Music and singing may appeal to you, too. However, your tendency to hop from one thing to another can prevent you from fulfilling your potential in anything.

Strengths: Flexibility, sensitivity, intuition, empathy, vocal abilities

Weaknesses: Emotional imbalance, inconsistency

How to use this amphibian's power: A frog can show you how to jump over problems instead of getting bogged down in your troubles. Ask a frog to help you provide emotional support to a friend in need. When you want to speak your piece or perform in public, a frog can teach you how to sing out boldly.

Symbolic meanings: If you encounter a frog outdoors or in a dream, it might advise you to speak up and verbalize your feelings. A frog's appearance could warn you to leap out of harm's way. Or, it may tell you to stop hopping about and get serious about something.

Gecko

Characteristics: With your exceptional powers of awareness, you sense everything that's going on around you and quickly pick up other people's "vibes"—you might even be psychic. Your sensitivity also lets you connect with your own inner wisdom, and when you follow it you usually come out ahead. Quick and agile, you easily move through life situations and can adapt to changing circumstances. You don't cling to outdated ideas or behaviors; instead, you put the past behind you and embrace new opportunities for growth.

Strengths: Awareness, inner wisdom, intuition, adaptability, agility

Weaknesses: Oversensitivity, flightiness, inconsistency

How to use this reptile's power: Do you need to let go of a painful issue from your past and get on with your life? If so, ask a gecko to show you how to shed what's holding you back and open up to new experiences. A gecko can also teach you how to get in touch with your intuition and expand your awareness.

Symbolic meanings: If a gecko appears in your waking or dreaming life, it may encourage you to be more detached and objective about an emotional situation. A gecko's appearance advises you to pay attention to your own inner knowing, rather than following the counsel of others. It can also warn you to keep your eyes open.

Gila Monster

Characteristics: Reclusive and secretive, you don't like being in public situations and prefer to withdraw to the quiet and safety of your own "burrow." Your desire to stay out of sight could lead you to seek an "undercover" career. Intrigued by what lies beneath the surface, you delve deeply into hidden matters and might be interested in research, psychology, or the occult. You tend to be slow moving and lethargic and may lack initiative. But once you sink your teeth into something, you hold on tight, and your tenacity enables you to accomplish your objectives. If someone crosses you or you feel threatened, you attack fiercely and can be a dangerous adversary.

Strengths: Tenacity, ability to delve deeply into matters, strong defenses

Weaknesses: Laziness, vindictiveness, antisocial behavior

How to use this reptile's power: When you need to get to the bottom of something, ask a Gila monster to assist you. A Gila monster can help you stand your ground and defend yourself.

Symbolic meanings: If you encounter a Gila monster in waking life or a dream, it might advise you to stay hidden and protect what's yours—don't reveal your ideas or feelings just yet. A Gila monster's appearance might warn that something is poisoning you; are your emotions or diet endangering your health?

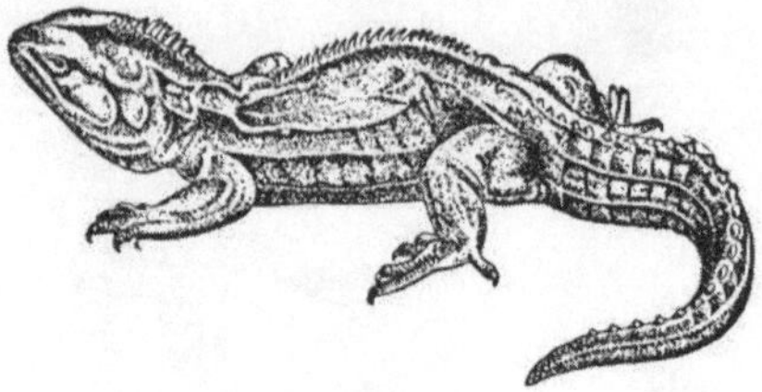

Iguana

Characteristics: An expert at survival, you've mastered the art of camouflage: you can melt into the crowd when you don't want to be seen, and know how to keep secrets. When danger threatens, you quickly scurry out of harm's way, like your speedy totem. Most of the time, however, you're comfortable with who you are and content with your everyday life. You're intensely aware of your environment and other people, but don't feel a need to judge or criticize. You can sit quietly, observing and enjoying your surroundings, without feeling pressured to do anything.

Strengths: Contentment, self-confidence, centeredness, acceptance

Weaknesses: Secretiveness, defensiveness

How to use this reptile's power: When your life seems out of control and stress is eating you up, let an iguana show you how to relax and just *be.* It can help you feel comfortable in your own skin and find contentment in your surroundings. An iguana resembles an earthy dragon; therefore it can also teach you how to ground and manage dragon power.

Symbolic meanings: The presence of an iguana in real life or a dream might tell you to slow down, get centered, and take it easy. It can also encourage you to enjoy where you are right now and find pleasure in little things. Sometimes an iguana's appearance warns you to stay out of sight for a while.

Komodo Dragon/Monitor Lizard

Characteristics: Known for your strength and aggressiveness, you pursue your goals with such ferocity that you can accomplish virtually anything. You don't feel a need to rush or pounce on opportunities; you patiently follow your dream until it's finally within your reach. However, you can be ruthless and might use questionable methods for obtaining what you desire. A formidable opponent, you have tremendous survival skills and don't back down from challenges.

Strengths: Determination, physical power

Weaknesses: Predatory nature, ruthlessness, indiscrimination

How to use this reptile's power: When you're faced with a daunting challenge or feel outnumbered, ask the fierce Komodo dragon to help you stand your ground. A Komodo dragon can also teach you how to strike out with certainty in order to get what you want: do what has to be done, without waffling.

Symbolic meanings: If you encounter a Komodo dragon in real life or dream of one, it can mean a change is imminent; take advantage of what's coming. It might also advise you to watch what you say and do, and to be more considerate of others. A Komodo dragon's appearance could warn you to beware of toxins in your diet or toxic people in your life who may be poisoning you.

Salamander

Characteristics: Like your totem, which can regrow lost limbs, you display tremendous resilience and powers of rejuvenation. If you suffer a loss or setback, you regroup and return stronger than ever. Your intuition, awareness, and flexibility keep you alert to changing conditions and help you adjust quickly if necessary. You're always updating yourself and have an uncanny ability to spot trends. Because the salamander lives in water, it is associated with emotional sensitivity and imagination, but Western magical traditions link it with the fire element. Your challenge, therefore, might be to balance inspiration and imagination, assertiveness and receptivity.

Strengths: Resilience, self-renewal, adaptability, intuition

Weaknesses: Slipperiness, emotional imbalance, inconsistency

How to use this amphibian's power: Have you lost something dear to you or been dealt a crushing blow? If so, a salamander can teach you the secrets of renewal and rebirth. A salamander can help you stay calm and on track during upsetting circumstances.

Symbolic meanings: If you spot a salamander in nature or a dream, it may warn that you'll experience a loss of some kind, but you'll be able to regain what you've lost in time. A salamander's appearance can also advise you to pay close attention to your environment and get ready for a change.

Sea Turtle

Characteristics: One of the oldest creatures on the planet, the turtle represents ancient wisdom and if this is your totem, you might be intrigued by history, archeology, or mythology. You possess superior survival skills and know how to protect and provide for yourself. Although you may appear cold or thick-skinned, underneath you're quite sensitive. Many of you are deeply emotional and intuitive. Most likely, you enjoy traveling, both in the physical world and in your imagination. Regardless of how far you wander, however, you still stay attached to your home and heritage, and family is important to you.

Strengths: Endurance, self-reliance, intuition

Weaknesses: Oversensitivity, defensiveness

How to use this reptile's power: A sea turtle can help you delve deeply into an area that you find confusing or frightening, perhaps one that's highly emotional. If you feel threatened or vulnerable, let this turtle show you how to take care of yourself or shore up your defenses.

Symbolic meanings: If you spot a sea turtle while you're awake or in a dream, it could be a sign that travel is in your future—perhaps a cruise or sailing excursion. A sea turtle might appear to warn you to protect yourself or to develop more self-sufficiency. It can also be a signal to strengthen connections to your home and family.

Snake (nonpoisonous)

Characteristics: The complicated and conflicting depictions of snakes in myth and lore echo your own complex nature. With this totem, you can be highly spiritual or underhanded and sinister—maybe a bit of both. The secrets of the ancients intrigue you, especially the mysteries of life, death, and rebirth, and you may possess healing gifts. You go through periodic transformations, during which you shed your old "skin" and create a new image of yourself. Regardless of how good-looking you are, you exude sexuality and other people may find you irresistible.

Strengths: Creative energy (kundalini), spirituality, wisdom, sexual prowess, healing power

Weaknesses: Duplicity, promiscuity

How to use this reptile's power: Would you like to enjoy a better sex life? A snake can teach you how to get in touch with kundalini power and let it awaken your sexual energy. If you're undergoing a time of transition or want to change something about yourself, ask a snake to guide you through a "rebirth."

Symbolic meanings: If you spot a nonpoisonous snake in the wild or a dream, it usually indicates a change is in store for you. A snake might also show up when your creative juices are awakening. When a snake appears, it can suggest that you examine your sex life: is it as rich and joyful as you'd like, or do you need to express your passion more fully?

Snake (poisonous)

Characteristics: You display many of the same traits as people with a nonpoisonous snake totem; however, you tend to be more aggressive and intense in everything you do. An extremist, you can rise to great heights or slip into dangerous or illicit activities. Quick and clever, you ardently pursue what you want in life, and when the time is right you strike with deadly precision. Your relationships tend to be passionate but also difficult; jealousy and vindictiveness could cause problems. Examine the unique features and behavior of various poisonous snakes to determine which is your totem: the beautiful coral snake? the powerful rattler? the wily asp? the majestic and magical cobra?

Strengths: Assertiveness, wisdom, healing power, sexual prowess, magical abilities

Weaknesses: Destructiveness, vindictiveness, cold-heartedness, debauchery

How to use this reptile's power: If you feel threatened or under attack, a snake can show you how to defend yourself without exposing yourself to harm. Ask a snake to help you quickly and decisively seize what you want. A snake can guide you to spiritual wisdom and reveal occult secrets. It can also teach you how to heal yourself, physically and emotionally.

Symbolic meanings: If a poisonous snake appears to you in real life or a dream, it can mean something is poisoning you—examine your emotions, behaviors, companions, and/or diet to discover what you need to change. A poisonous snake might appear when something in your life is about to die (figuratively) and transform you in some way. It can also tell you to be more loving, considerate, and forgiving in a relationship.

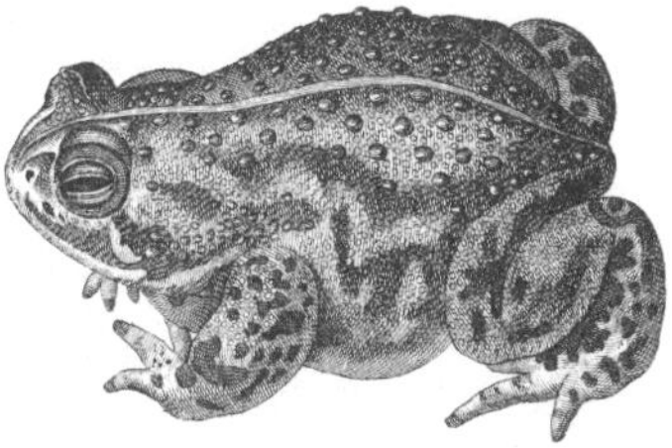

Toad

Characteristics: You share some qualities with people who have a frog totem; however, you're less emotional and more practical. Instead of simply dreaming about what you want, you use your resourcefulness to bring ideas down to earth. When problems arise, you leap over them; when opportunities come your way, you jump on them. Sometimes, however, you hop from one thing to another and may lack patience or persistence. In mythology, toads symbolize luck, and you might be blessed with good fortune. Perhaps you love singing or public speaking and have a strong voice, though not necessarily a melodious one.

Strengths: Flexibility, resourcefulness, good luck, vocal abilities

Weaknesses: Inconsistency, lack of imagination

How to use this amphibian's power: When undergoing a change, let a toad show you how to use your inner knowing and resourcefulness to stay grounded and make the best of it. A toad can help you hop out of a situation in which you feel bored or bogged down. If you've experienced a period of bad luck, ask a toad to change it for you.

Symbolic meanings: Seeing a toad in its habitat or in one of your dreams can mean your luck is about to change for the better. A toad's appearance may indicate that an opportunity is coming and to jump on it. Or, it might warn you to stop hopping about: choose a path and stick to it.

Tortoise

Characteristics: This reptile bears many similar qualities to the sea turtle, including highly developed protection skills and self-reliance. You're quite resourceful and few adversaries get the better of you. Persistent and patient, you know how to take it slow and easy rather than burning yourself out; in the end, you usually reach your destination successfully. Your heritage and home are very important to you; if you travel, you might enjoy RVing. Because the tortoise is one of the oldest species on earth and known for its longevity, people who have it as a totem may enjoy a long life.

Strengths: Endurance, resourcefulness, patience, determination

Weaknesses: Sluggishness, lack of imagination, insensitivity

How to use this reptile's power: When you feel stressed out or overwhelmed by life's pressures, ask a tortoise to help you slow down and take it one step at a time. This reptile can also teach you how to protect yourself and your home from harm.

Symbolic meanings: If you see a tortoise while awake or dreaming, it may advise you to pace yourself and stop rushing around. On the other hand, it can recommend that you're not moving quickly enough and need to pick up your pace. A tortoise might also suggest that you look to the past for answers.

Worm Lizard

Characteristics: This creature is categorized as a squamate, and is related to snakes and lizards. It spends nearly all its life underground. If this is your totem, you, too, may prefer to stay out of sight much of the time and might be a recluse. The ordinary, everyday world doesn't interest you—instead, you seek to understand the hidden realms and might be drawn to psychology, spiritual studies, or occult knowledge. A job that lets you work behind the scenes or undercover would probably appeal to you. Like the worm lizard that tunnels deep into the earth, you could also excel in excavation, mining, building underground structures such as subways, or research. Although your vision may not be especially good, you might have exceptional hearing and sense of touch.

Strengths: Persistence, insight, sensitivity

Weaknesses: Reclusiveness, lack of imagination

How to use this creature's power: If you need to find out what's going on beneath the surface, ask a worm lizard to help you dig deeply until you discover the truth. A worm lizard can also teach you determination and help you stay focused on a long-term project.

Symbolic meanings: If you see a worm lizard while awake or dreaming, it could be a sign that you need to delve more deeply into a situation. Sometimes this creature's appearance can advise you to use all your senses, including your intuition—what you see might not be accurate. A worm lizard might also warn you to stay out of sight for a while.

"Fish have the power to take us into lands of fantasy—they let our analytical minds drop out of sight and allow our imaginations to roam the seas of our thoughts for awhile."

—Avia Venefica, *www.whats-your-sign.com*

Fish and Sea Creatures

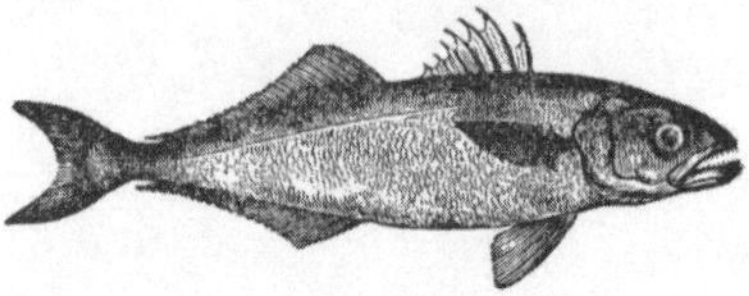

Bluefish

Characteristics: Your "take no prisoners" style makes you a fierce competitor, whether you're on the playing field or in the boardroom. Once you decide to go after something, you let nothing stop you. You snap up opportunities that come your way and quickly make the most of them. Your ambition knows no bounds, however, and you never seem to get enough. You'll join forces with other like-minded individuals in order to accomplish a goal, but your combative nature can make it hard to maintain long-term cooperative ventures. With your physical strength and speed, you could be a good athlete and might excel at swimming, boating, or other water sports. A career in the military could suit you well, too.

Strengths: Physical power, speed, determination, assertiveness

Weaknesses: Aggressiveness, destructiveness, ruthlessness, mob/gang behavior

How to use this fish's power: When you want to accomplish something fast, a bluefish can show you how to strike with speed and certainty. A bluefish can help you overcome fears or reservations, and to bite through problems.

Symbolic meanings: If you see a bluefish in waking life or a dream, it may advise you to be more determined or aggressive. Conversely, it could mean you're behaving in a cutthroat or ruthless manner.

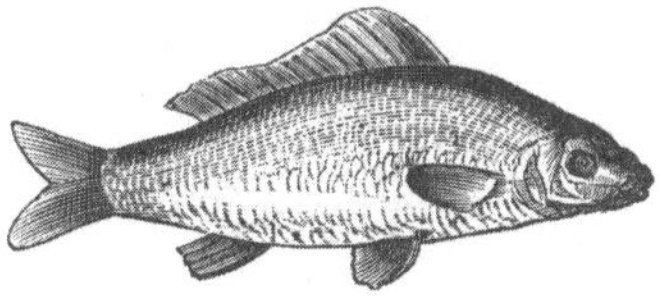

Carp

Characteristics: Adaptable and resourceful, you easily adjust to whatever circumstances you find yourself in and make the best of situations. Your hardy nature allows you to manage in all sorts of conditions, and you're willing to do whatever is necessary in order to get along. Perhaps you come from an immigrant family and have learned to make your way in a different culture. You don't mind working hard or getting your hands dirty, and your tenacity can help you prosper. However, you have a tendency to stir things up and may agitate others who feel you're moving into their territory. At some time during your life, you might relocate to a place far from your birth.

Strengths: Adaptability, hardiness, tenacity, versatility

Weaknesses: Lack of discrimination, lack of clarity

How to use this fish's power: If you're new in town or just feel out of place, let a carp show you how to adapt. Would you like to visit another country? Invite a carp to come along as your traveling companion.

Symbolic meanings: Spot a carp while awake or dream of one and it can mean you're stirring up a lot of muck or irritating others. In a murky situation, it's hard to see clearly. Sometimes this fish's appearance can advise you to stop "carping" about something and be more accepting.

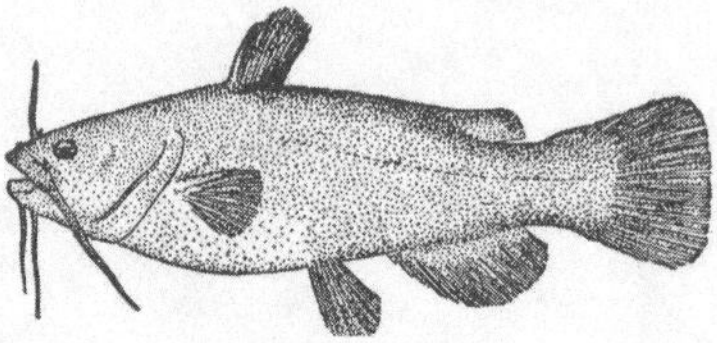

Catfish

Characteristics: Discriminating, you know what's good for you and what isn't, and don't waste time with nonessentials. Nor do you surround yourself with people who might drag you down. Emotionally sensitive, you seek a comfortable existence without a lot of upsets. You go with the flow instead of wasting time battling the currents. However, you can be lazy and may simply wait for things to come your way, rather than trying to achieve a higher position or lifestyle.

Strengths: Discernment, awareness, practicality

Weaknesses: Laziness, oversensitivity, lack of motivation

How to use this fish's power: Are you cluttering up your home with too much stuff? Are you associating with the wrong sort of people? A catfish can teach you how to be more discriminating. It can also help you stop struggling and go with the flow.

Symbolic meanings: If you see a catfish in real life or a dream, it may advise you to stop wallowing in the "mud" and seek higher ground, physically, socially, or spiritually. This fish's appearance can also mean you need to sort out what's really important to you and what's not—get rid of things that no longer serve you and that might be keeping you stuck in old patterns.

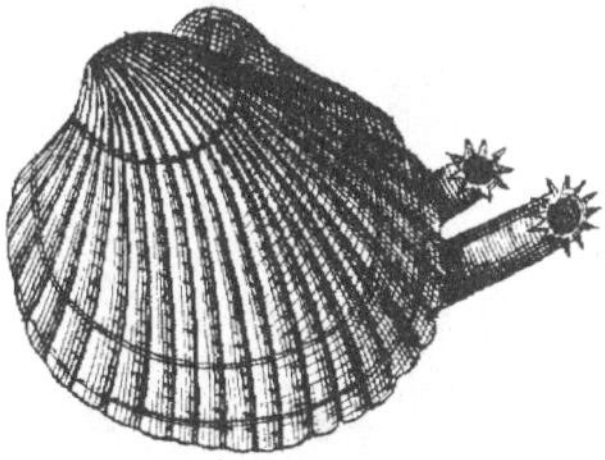

Clam

Characteristics: Quiet, emotional, and reserved, you don't say much and usually keep to yourself instead of seeking the company of others. You feel you have everything you need within yourself. Highly intuitive, you align yourself with the rhythms around you and patiently wait until the time is right to make your move. Your tough outer shell conceals your inner sensitivity and protects you from life's hardships; few people realize how gentle and tenderhearted you really are. However, you have trouble expressing your feelings and tend to "clam up" rather than sharing your inner gifts with the world.

Strengths: Intuition, kindness, sensitivity, patience, resourcefulness

Weaknesses: Emotional imbalance, secretiveness, defensiveness

How to use this creature's power: A clam can help you to be patient and to judge the "waters" around you, so you can act at the right time. A clam can also show you how turn inward for answers and to appreciate your own resources. Let a clam teach you the value of silence.

Symbolic meanings: If you see a clam while awake or dream about one, it might mean you're isolating yourself and hiding behind a thick shell because you feel vulnerable. A clam's appearance can also advise you to "clam up" and not reveal something.

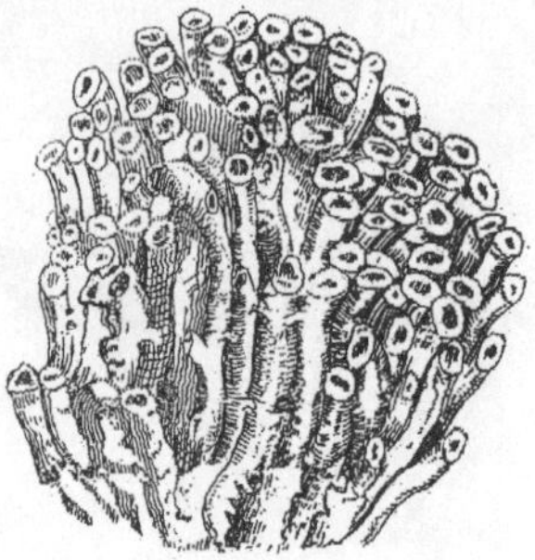

Coral

Characteristics: Coral reefs comprise only 1 percent of aquatic life, but support 25 percent of it. If this is your totem, you, too, provide shelter, protection, and nourishment for many others. You generously share your resources with all who seek them. Your strong personal foundation and structured lifestyle enable you to withstand even turbulent conditions, and to serve as a role model in your community. But even though you may seem rigid, you intuit the rhythms and currents in life, and adapt to its ebb and flow. You create your own world, and you do it beautifully.

Strengths: Structure, nourishing nature, creativity, generosity, stability

Weaknesses: Self-sacrifice, immobility

How to use this creature's power: Are you seeking shelter from life's storms? If so, a coral reef can provide a safe haven for you. Coral can also teach you the value of structure and help you establish stability in your personal or professional life. From coral, you can learn how to create something of lasting beauty and value.

Symbolic meanings: If you spy a coral reef while awake or dreaming, it might warn you to protect or nourish yourself. It can also suggest that you stabilize your resources or establish a firmer foundation. You might see coral when you need to express your creativity more productively.

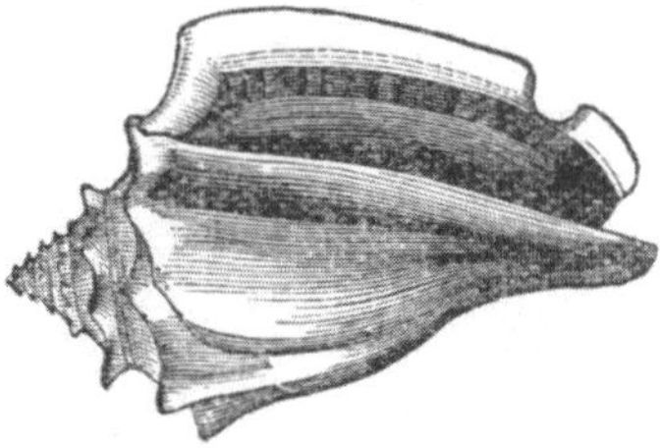

Conch

Characteristics: The conch is a large sea snail, most noted for its shell. In Greek myth, Poseidon's son Triton blew a conch shell to calm the seas. If the conch is your totem, you capably handle emotional ups and downs, and can bring order in turbulent situations. Honest and forthright, you speak the truth—whether or not people want to hear it—and could be a wise teacher, spiritual leader, or prophet. You call other people to the right action and can inspire them to follow a more harmonious or correct path in life. Perhaps you're blessed with musical ability and might enjoy playing a trumpet or other wind instrument.

Strengths: Emotional balance, honesty, foresight, wisdom, inspiration, musical ability

Weaknesses: Pride, tactlessness

How to use this creature's power: A conch can help you find your own voice and speak out when you need to. Ask a conch to assist you with learning to play a musical instrument or giving a performance. A conch can also guide you through emotional upsets.

Symbolic meanings: If you see a conch in a dream or spot one in its natural habitat, it might be a wake-up call. A conch's spiral shape may recommend following a spiritual path. It could also advise you to speak out honestly about something or to sound an alert. In some cases, it might tell you not to "blow your own horn."

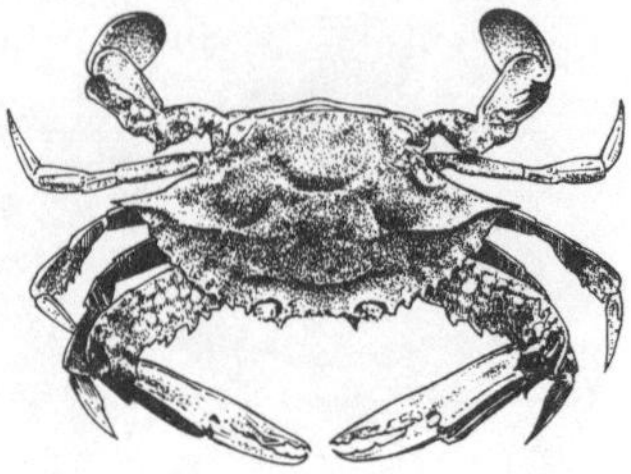

Crab

Characteristics: Your tough, spiky exterior conceals your sensitive nature and your deep emotions. Shy and reclusive, you withdraw from the pressures of the outer world and hide in your shell. When you feel threatened, however, you may snap with surprising force and sharpness. Like people born under the zodiac sign Cancer, whose symbol is the crab, your movement through life is never straight; instead, taking an indirect path will lead you to your goals. You prefer to sidestep challenges rather than approach them head on. Cancer is ruled by the moon, and you might find your moods change with the moon's phases.

Strengths: Adaptability, self-preservation, intuition

Weaknesses: Oversensitivity, irritability, reclusiveness, defensiveness

How to use this creature's power: When a direct route is blocked, ask a crab to show you how to take a different path in order to reach your goal. If you feel attacked, a crab can teach you the fine art of self-protection.

Symbolic meanings: If you encounter a crab in its natural habitat or a dream, it may warn you to protect yourself. A crab can also advise you to come out of your shell instead of withdrawing from the world. Sometimes a crab's appearance means you're being "crabby" and need to balance your emotions.

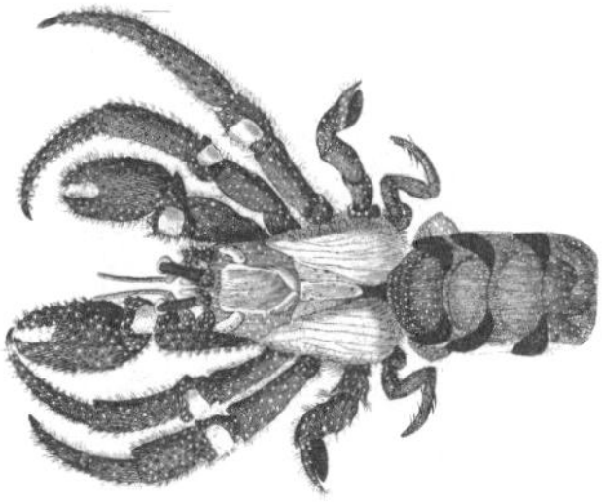

Crayfish

Characteristics: Shy and reclusive, you scurry away from the public eye and hesitate to shine light into situations that you find murky or intimidating. You're inclined to hide from things that frighten or upset you, instead of facing them squarely. But if you really want something, you're willing to fight for it. You're smart enough, however, to back out of situations that might be detrimental to you rather than taking unnecessary risks. When you do suffer a loss, you learn from your mistakes and regroup, growing stronger from the experience.

Strengths: Ability to recover from losses, cleverness

Weaknesses: Secretiveness, reclusiveness

How to use this creature's power: A crayfish can show you how to back out of a bad deal or unpleasant situation without losing face. If you want to avoid unwanted attention or publicity, ask a crayfish to help you hide until the threat blows over.

Symbolic meanings: If you see a crayfish in its natural habitat or dream about one, it might advise you to stop wallowing in the mud. It could also recommend backing down from a fight instead of escalating a conflict. Sometimes a crawfish shows up to encourage you to stop doubting yourself and move forward.

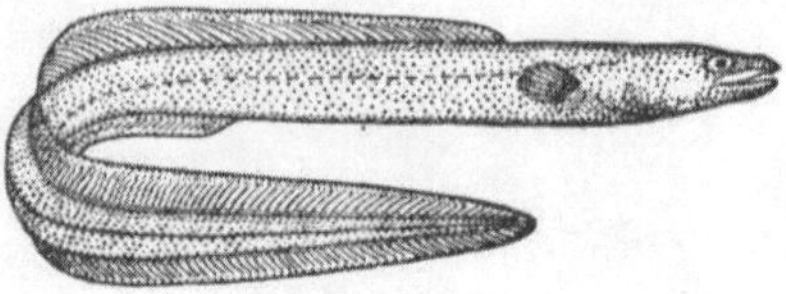

Eel

Characteristics: If the eel is your totem, you share some traits with people who have a snake totem, including a powerful sexuality and the ability to tap into the creative life force known as kundalini energy. You navigate the waters of life with ease and flexibility, and have a knack for slipping out of difficult situations. Shy, sensitive, and secretive, you don't call attention to yourself, and can be elusive if someone tries to get too close to you. The mysteries of life and death intrigue you, as do the hidden realms of the unconscious and the occult. Consequently, you might pursue a career in psychology, metaphysics, or healing.

Strengths: Sexual attractiveness, vitality, flexibility, intuition

Weaknesses: Slipperiness, secretiveness, elusiveness

How to use this creature's power: Do you want to improve your sex life or be more sexually attractive? Ask an eel to share its secrets with you. An eel can also guide you on a journey into the hidden realms to uncover occult mysteries.

Symbolic meanings: If you see an eel in its natural habitat or a dream, it might signal an awakening sexuality or encourage you to get in touch with your feelings about intimacy. An eel's appearance could also warn you to hide from prying eyes or to keep quiet about something.

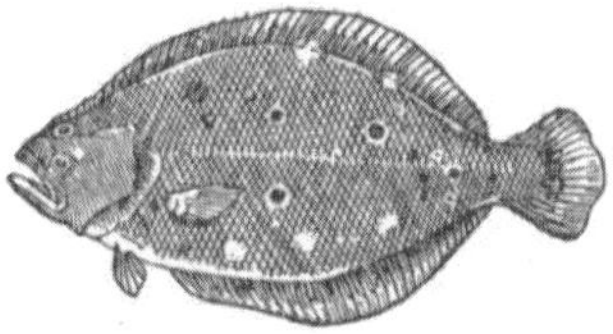

Flounder/Sole

Characteristics: A master of camouflage, you don't like to draw attention to yourself or stand out in a crowd. Instead, you prefer to wield power behind the scenes. Shy and sensitive, you usually wait for people to come to you instead of initiating relationships. Nor do you actively seek out career or financial opportunities; rather, you quietly and intently observe what's going on around you until you see something you want, then you grab it. Your ability to stay grounded during stressful circumstances is one of your most notable assets.

Strengths: Pragmatism, groundedness, good observation skills, patience

Weaknesses: Secretiveness, aloofness, lack of ambition

How to use this fish's power: A flounder or sole can teach you how to be patient and take your time with a project or process, instead of rushing things. It can also show you how to conceal your intentions when you don't want others to know what you're doing.

Symbolic meanings: If you spot a flounder or sole while awake or in one of your dreams, it could recommend waiting for something you want to come to you instead of forcing it. It might also advise you to stop feeding at the bottom and ascend to a higher level. Sometimes a flounder's appearance can warn you that a venture or relationship you're involved in is about to "flounder."

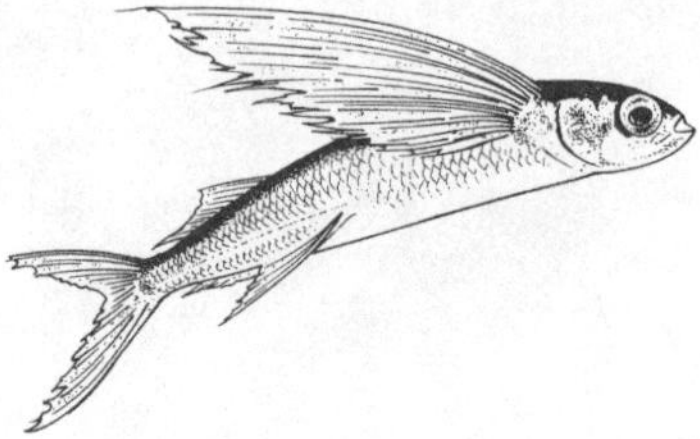

Flying Fish

Characteristics: Unlike many people with fish totems, you don't let your emotions distort your thinking. You can remain detached when difficult emotional situations occur and examine things from an intellectual perspective. Even though you set your sights high, you believe in yourself and your abilities—for you, the sky is the limit. You're not afraid to take what appear to be leaps of faith, because your intuition and insight enable you to see beyond the present moment and you trust higher forces to guide you. By balancing mind, emotions, and spirit, you can soar above past limitations.

Strengths: Intuition, intelligence, emotional balance, clarity

Weaknesses: Escapism, idealism

How to use this fish's power: A flying fish can show you how to soar above emotional troubles and gain an intellectual or spiritual perspective. When you need to escape danger, ask a flying fish to help you fly out of harm's way. Let a flying fish guide you when you take a leap of faith.

Symbolic meanings: If you spot a flying fish while awake or dreaming, it may advise you to stay detached during an emotional situation and rise above troubled waters. It might also suggest that you fly higher: reach for a loftier goal instead of sticking with what's familiar.

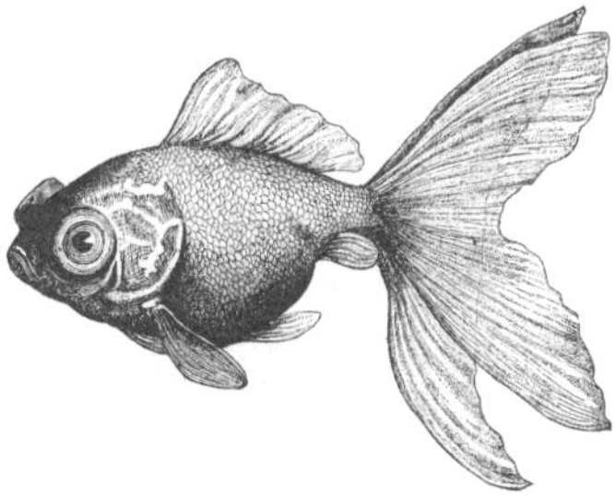

Goldfish/Koi

Characteristics: The Chinese consider the goldfish a symbol of good luck and prosperity, and often display them in their homes and businesses. Like this sparkling totem, you attract good fortune in all you do, perhaps because of your optimism, sunny nature, and sociability. You expect good things to happen, and they do. You keep an open mind, and your keen perceptual abilities let you spot opportunities everywhere. With your creativity, imagination, and business acumen, you know how to turn those opportunities into success stories.

Strengths: Good luck, optimism, cheerful personality, perception, business savvy

Weaknesses: Idealism, naiveté

How to use this fish's power: Could you use some good luck? Of course you can, so ask a goldfish to bring fortune and fame your way. A goldfish can also show you how to make the most of opportunities and to see possibilities that other people overlook.

Symbolic meanings: Seeing a goldfish in waking life or a dream can mean good luck is coming your way. It can also tell you to be on the alert for new treasures or benefits, perhaps in places you hadn't expected. Sometimes when a goldfish appears it urges you to lighten up and be more cheerful—life is good.

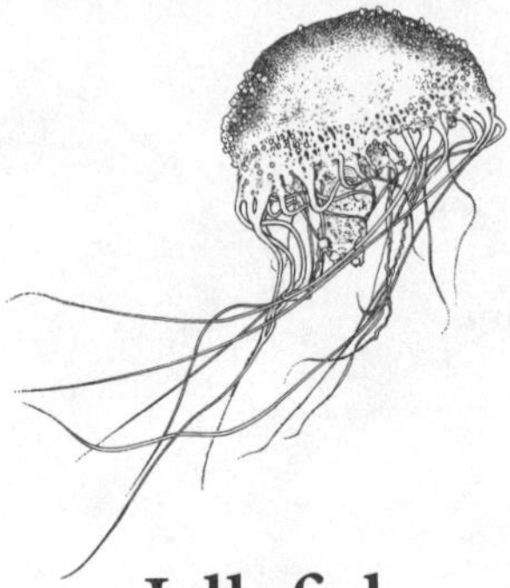

Jellyfish

Characteristics: If the jellyfish is your totem, "go with the flow" might be your motto. Your unpretentious, easygoing nature enables you to adapt to conditions and get along in almost any circumstance. You trust the universe to guide you and let matters take their course instead of trying to force them. Open and even transparent in your dealings with other people, you don't try to disguise yourself or your intentions. However, because you're so forthright you sometimes say things that sting others, without meaning to cause harm.

Strengths: Honesty, lack of artifice, flexibility, easygoing personality

Weaknesses: Tactlessness, naiveté, laziness

How to use this creature's power: During stressful circumstances, ask a jellyfish to help you relax, be flexible, and take it easy. A jellyfish can teach you how to trust your own inner wisdom or higher powers. If something painful from your past still stings, a jellyfish can help you let go of the hurt and move on.

Symbolic meanings: If a jellyfish appears to you, whether in waking life or a dream, it might encourage you to stop striving and just go with the flow. Trust that things will work out in due time. A jellyfish could also warn you to be careful what you reveal of yourself. Speak diplomatically, instead of being brutally honest.

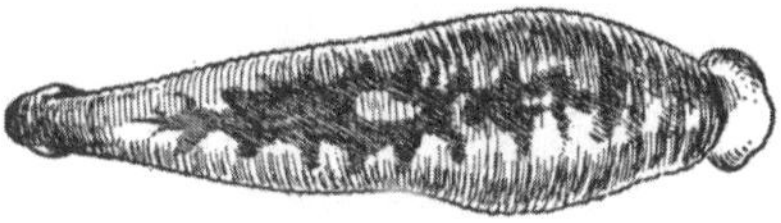

Leech

Characteristics: You know how to be patient and wait for good things to come to you. That doesn't mean you're lazy, however; quite the opposite. Once you've chosen a path, you pursue it with quiet determination, and you trust that whatever you undertake will yield rewards. During stressful situations, you remain calm and centered. Your persistence enables you to gain from both personal relationships and professional endeavors. However, you can be an opportunist and "feed" on others in order to get what you want.

Strengths: Patience, persistence, self-confidence

Weaknesses: Opportunism, selfishness

How to use this creature's power: A leech can teach you how to draw sustenance from any situation. If you're the impatient type, ask a leech to help you develop more focus and determination. Are you too self-sacrificing? If you tend to give too much of yourself to other people, a leech can show you how to nourish yourself first.

Symbolic meanings: If you see a leech while awake or dreaming, it might recommend purging something that's unhealthy from your life, or undergoing a purification treatment to eliminate toxins from your body. A leech's appearance could mean something or someone is leeching your vitality; or, conversely, that you are leeching off someone else.

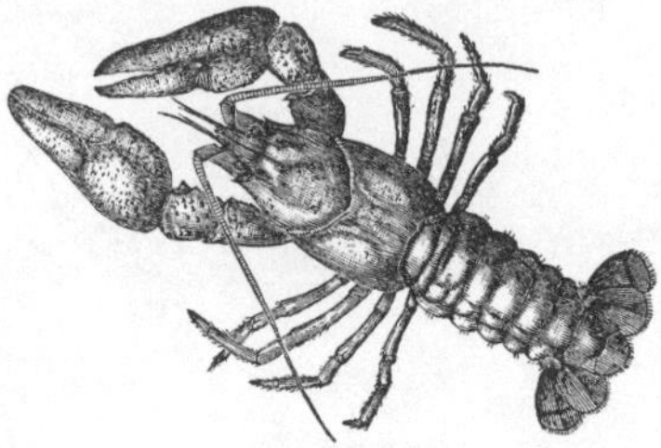

Lobster

Characteristics: Self-preservation is one of your foremost considerations, and you're very good at it. Your hard outer shell protects you from unpleasant or harmful circumstances. However, it also prevents other people from getting close to you. You quickly move forward to seize what you desire and clamp onto it with a vise-like grip. But if things don't turn out as you'd hoped, you retreat just as quickly in order to cut your losses and save face. Your amazing powers of rejuvenation enable you to recover from setbacks and to keep growing stronger year after year.

Strengths: Self-preservation, cleverness, good reflexes, rejuvenation

Weaknesses: Defensiveness, aggressiveness, indecision

How to use this creature's power: A lobster can teach you how to defend yourself, and to understand when to attack and when to retreat. If you've suffered a loss or defeat, ask a lobster to help you learn from the experience and rebuild.

Symbolic meanings: A lobster may warn you to protect yourself. If you see one in real life or a dream, it might also point out that by hiding behind a hard shell, you're cutting yourself off from the joys of life. Sometimes a lobster's appearance can presage a loss, but it also assures you that you'll survive and grow stronger in the future.

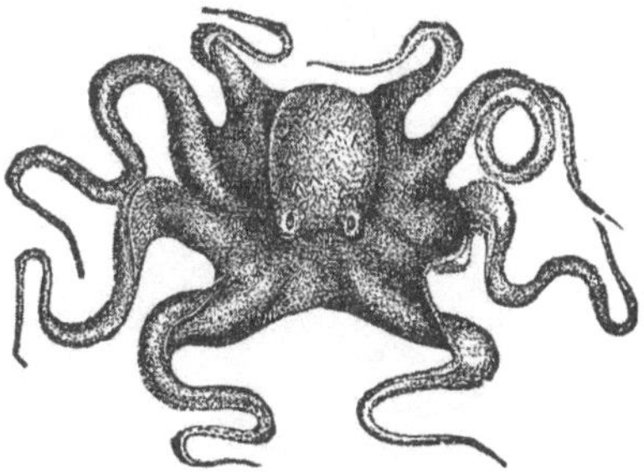

Octopus

Characteristics: You move through life with grace and flexibility, and can maneuver around obstacles without getting thrown off course. That's because you stay emotionally grounded, even while exploring mysterious realms or journeying through new experiences. You're also blessed with intuition and insight that can alert you to threats and guide you through the murky waters of life. You reach out eagerly for what you want and once you've grasped it, you hold on tight. Versatile and curious, you reach for a lot of things and risk getting involved in so many projects and activities that you lose your focus.

Strengths: Adaptability, groundedness, intuition, versatility

Weaknesses: Slipperiness, inconsistency, clinginess

How to use this creature's power: When you encounter an obstacle in your path, ask an octopus to guide you gracefully around it. An octopus can also show you how to get out of tight spots and to stay hidden when you don't want to attract attention.

Symbolic meanings: If you see an octopus while awake or in a dream, it may mean you're trying to grasp too much and need to let go of something. It might also advise you to stay grounded during an emotionally turbulent time. Sometimes an octopus appears when you need to adapt to changes and be more fluid.

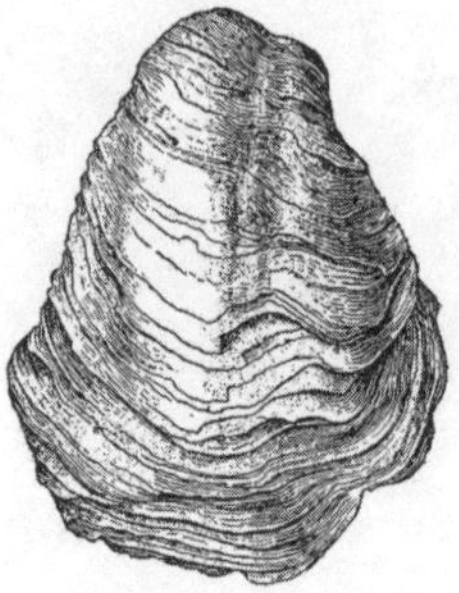

Oyster

Characteristics: You rely on your intuition to help you sense the surrounding currents and discern what's valuable or potentially harmful to you. This resource enables you to protect and nurture yourself. Like people with the clam totem, you hide your tender emotions behind a tough outer shell to keep from getting hurt. However, by opening up to experiences in the outer world, you can discover many wonderful things that you wouldn't have been privy to otherwise. One of your life lessons is to take the irritations and challenges life presents and transform them into "pearls."

Strengths: Discernment, inner wisdom, intuition, creativity, resourcefulness

Weaknesses: Oversensitivity, emotional imbalance, defensiveness

How to use this creature's power: An oyster can teach you how to learn from life, and to make the best of even difficult experiences. It can also help you to become more discriminating and to stay balanced emotionally, instead of letting little things irritate you.

Symbolic meanings: An oyster, whether in real life or a dream, may advise you to balance your inner and outer worlds, instead of isolating yourself. An oyster's appearance could also encourage you to learn and grow from a painful experience, and to find something of value in it.

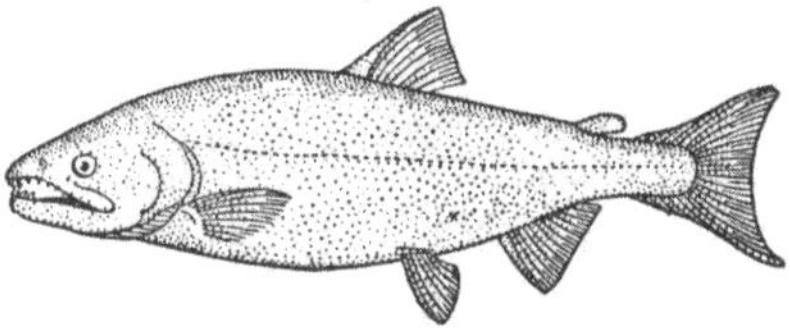

Salmon

Characteristics: You possess a strong will and sense of adventure—you aren't afraid to face a challenge. You eagerly pursue risky or even dangerous undertakings, fearless in the face of obstacles, confident you'll succeed even against great odds. Dynamic, graceful, and energetic, you probably enjoy sports and/or other physical activities that require strength and speed. Many people with the salmon totem like to travel, and you may journey long distances in your quest for excitement; however, you always maintain close ties to your home and family.

Strengths: Courage, strength, agility, self-confidence

Weaknesses: Willfulness, recklessness, combativeness

How to use this fish's power: When you face a challenge or problem, ask a salmon to show you how best to deal with it. This fish can give you confidence and determination when you feel scared, uncertain, or weak. If you're going on a trip, invite a salmon to come along—you're sure to have a memorable adventure.

Symbolic meanings: If you see a salmon or dream of one, it may urge you to be more daring. Take charge of your life and don't let obstacles deter you from your goal. A salmon might also herald the start of a journey or a new path in life. Sometimes a salmon reminds you not to lose touch with your roots.

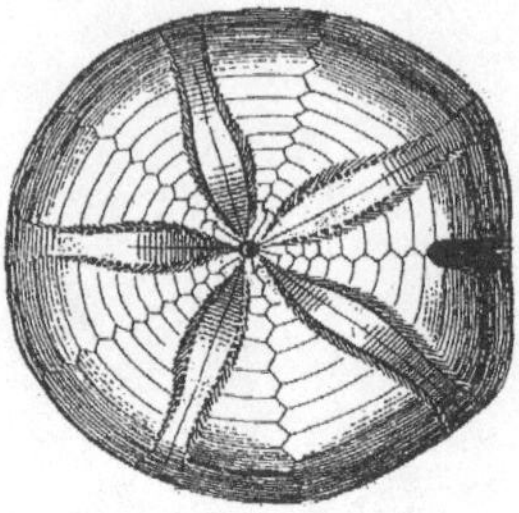

Sand Dollar

Characteristics: In Christianity, the distinctive pattern on the sand dollar's shell represents Christ's crucifixion wounds, and the tiny "doves" inside the shell signify hope. If this is your totem, you may devote yourself to a spiritual path even though following that path might require self-sacrifice. The sand dollar's five-petaled design also signifies the physical body and your strong connection with it, as well as your keen senses. Balancing body, emotions, and spirit could be one of your life lessons—you might even choose a career in holistic healing. You remain hopeful in all you do and can bring hope to others as well.

Strengths: Spirituality, inspiration, devotion, healing power

Weaknesses: Emotional instability, idealism, self-sacrifice

How to use this creature's power: If you're on a spiritual journey, or want to begin one, a sand dollar can help you navigate the ups and downs along the way. A sand dollar can also teach you how to balance body, mind, emotions, and spirit in order to heal yourself.

Symbolic meanings: If you see a sand dollar in waking life or in a dream, it could mean you are resurrecting yourself after a trauma or loss. Its appearance encourages you to remain hopeful. It might also recommend balancing your physical body and emotions in order to promote healing, or perhaps to consider holistic therapies.

Sea Anemone

Characteristics: Your beauty and colorful nature attract others to you—all you have to do is be yourself. Patient, flexible, and intuitive, you know how to "gauge the waters" and trust the universe to provide what you need. You stay balanced and centered through life's ebbs and flows, gracefully adapting to circumstances instead of resisting. By remaining observant, you gain wisdom from each person and situation you encounter, and store it for use later on.

Strengths: Beauty, patience, awareness, adaptability

Weaknesses: Lack of ambition, laziness, idealism

How to use this creature's power: A sea anemone can show you how to stop struggling and be patient—trust the process. During stressful times, a sea anemone can help you balance your emotions so that you don't lose your center. A sea anemone can also teach you how to flaunt your beauty in order to attract other people.

Symbolic meanings: If you see a sea anemone in nature or in a dream, it might warn you to be observant and cautious, instead of taking action. Be patient. Let people and opportunities come to you. A sea anemone's appearance could also recommend using your intuition to interpret a situation—things might not be what they seem.

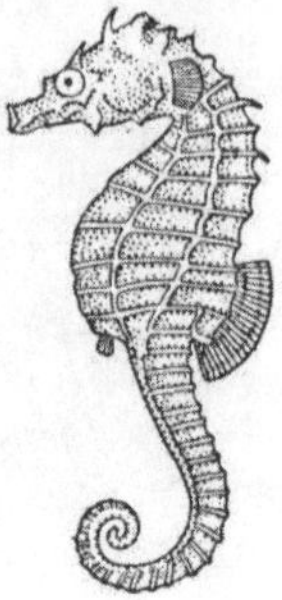

Sea Horse

Characteristics: Both the ancient Greeks and the Chinese considered the sea horse a symbol of good luck. Other people might view you as lucky, and indeed, you may enjoy good fortune in life. But your "luck" comes partly from being patient, persistent, and cheerful in all you do. You don't waste energy rushing after wealth and fame, or trying to impress others; you're content with who you are and you make the most of what life brings you. Protective of those you love, men with this totem in particular display strong nurturing qualities and make wonderful parents.

Strengths: Patience, acceptance, good luck, cheerfulness, nurturing nature

Weaknesses: Rigidity, laziness, lack of ambition

How to use this fish's power: Could you use some good luck? Ask a sea horse to bring good fortune your way. A sea horse can also show you how to be patient and not rush something; you'll be more successful if you take your time and do the job right.

Symbolic meanings: A sea horse, spotted while awake or dreaming, could be a sign that good luck is on its way. Sometimes a sea horse's appearance recommends nurturing yourself or someone else. It might also advise you to take things easy, be more accepting, and just enjoy life.

Sea Urchin

Characteristics: Your bristly exterior hides your tender interior, and few people realize how gentle and sensitive you truly are. Deeply emotional, you try to protect yourself against real or imagined hurts by keeping others at bay. Learning to discern what is good for you and what's harmful is one of your challenges. You proceed through life slowly, patiently, and methodically; even during turbulent situations, you stay grounded and centered and don't get swept away by upsets or changes.

Strengths: Patience, balance, good protection, ability to remain centered

Weaknesses: Defensiveness, oversensitivity, prickliness

How to use this creature's power: During emotionally challenging circumstances, a sea urchin can help you remain centered. If you feel vulnerable and in need of protection, a sea urchin can teach you the art of self-defense. It can also help you understand when to be tough and when to be tender.

Symbolic meanings: If you spot a sea urchin, it may mean you're being too prickly and defensive, whether you see it in real life or a dream. Stop bristling and don't take offense over something immaterial. A sea urchin might appear to guide you slowly and patiently through an emotional situation. Observe the urchin's color for further clues to its meaning.

Shark

Characteristics: You go after what you want with great strength, speed, and determination—you can accomplish anything you set out to do. Fiercely competitive, you enjoy challenges and easily overcome adversaries. You seem to have a sixth sense when it comes to finding an opponent's weakness. You can be ruthless, however, and may subscribe to the belief that might makes right. In order to be happy and healthy, you need to stay active; for you, boredom is the kiss of death. You could succeed as an athlete, venture capitalist, entrepreneur, stockbroker, or in the military.

Strengths: Physical power, speed, determination, ambition

Weaknesses: Ruthlessness, unscrupulousness

How to use this fish's power: A shark's strength and ferociousness can help you overcome seemingly impossible odds or to achieve a goal that appears beyond your capabilities. In a competition, a shark can give you an edge over the opposition. It can also help you protect yourself against an attack.

Symbolic meanings: If you see a shark in real life or a dream, it may warn you that an attack is likely—stay alert and on guard. Conversely, it could advise you to attack with speed and sureness. Sometimes its appearance means you're behaving like a shark and need to be more considerate of others.

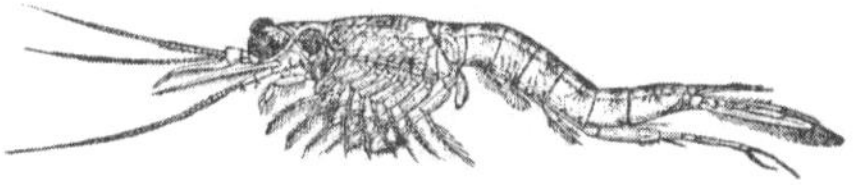

Shrimp/Prawn

Characteristics: Solitary and shy, you often shun social situations and tend to hide in your shell instead of asserting yourself in the world. However, your versatility allows you to adapt to whatever situation your find yourself in and to navigate the waters of life with agility. In part, you succeed because you intuitively know when to move forward and when to back off. You go with the flow, instead of bucking the tide. Your highly developed perception also enables you to sense when danger is afoot and retreat or hide quickly.

Strengths: Versatility, adaptability, agility, perceptiveness

Weaknesses: Defensiveness, withdrawal from others

How to use this creature's power: A shrimp can teach you how to pick your battles, and to back away from a fight that you can't win. It can also show you how to maneuver gracefully through tricky situations and relationships. Ask a shrimp to guide you when making investments or business decisions: it can advise you when to take action and when to pull back.

Symbolic meanings: If you see a shrimp while awake or dream of one, it may mean you're hiding in your shell and need to be more outgoing. It's okay to take a few, calculated risks—let your senses guide you. A shrimp's appearance could also advise you to be flexible emotionally.

Snail

Characteristics: Patient and disciplined, you proceed through life at a slow, steady pace. Rather than getting stressed out by the bumps in life, you glide smoothly over obstacles. You keep your feet on the ground and don't hold unrealistic expectations. A homebody, you enjoy the quiet comforts of domestic life instead of seeking excitement or lots of social activity. Although you tend to be reclusive and self-protective, not wanting to expose yourself to potential harm, you know when to come out of your shell and take steps to get what you want.

Strengths: Patience, steadiness, persistence, serenity

Weaknesses: Sluggishness, lack of imagination, defensiveness

How to use this creature's power: A snail can teach you how to take your time and pace yourself, in order to move easily through life. Let a snail guide you smoothly over rough spots, without losing your footing. Do you tend to be too idealistic? Ask a snail to help you stay grounded as you pursue your objectives.

Symbolic meanings: If you see a snail in real life or a dream, it may warn you to move more quickly instead of at a snail's pace. Conversely, it might advise you to slow down and stop racing around, wasting your energy.

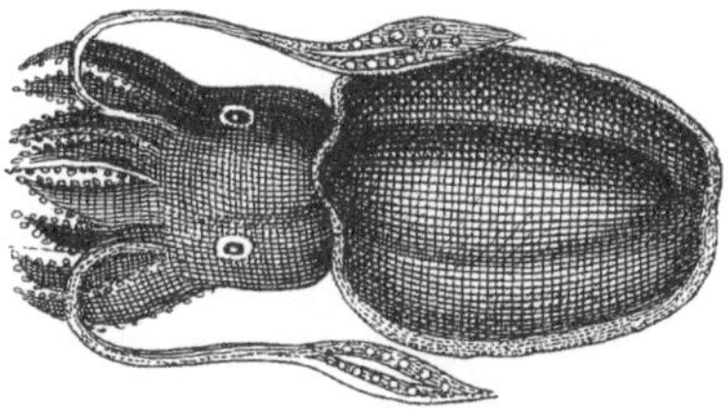

Squid

Characteristics: You share some similarities with people who have an octopus totem, but you're more imaginative and less grounded. With your sensitivity to light and color, you could excel as an artist, fashion designer, or interior decorator. Graceful and flexible, you glide through life with agility, and skirt problems instead of letting them weigh you down. You're very sensitive to other people, too, and can sense what they're thinking or feeling. Your intuition lets you gauge situations in order to make your move or to protect yourself. Instead of focusing on superficial matters, you seek deeper truths and might be interested in spiritual topics.

Strengths: Imagination, grace, agility, intuition, good defenses

Weaknesses: Fearfulness, idealism, inconsistency

How to use this creature's power: A squid can give you inspiration for an artistic project and help you infuse it with emotional depth and beauty. When faced with an obstacle, ask a squid to guide you around it and into smoother waters. A squid can also teach you the art of concealment when you want to avoid attention.

Symbolic meanings: If you encounter a squid in the waking world or a dream, it may warn you to stay out of sight or to keep your intentions secret. A squid might show up to encourage you to use your imagination or to express yourself in an artistic way.

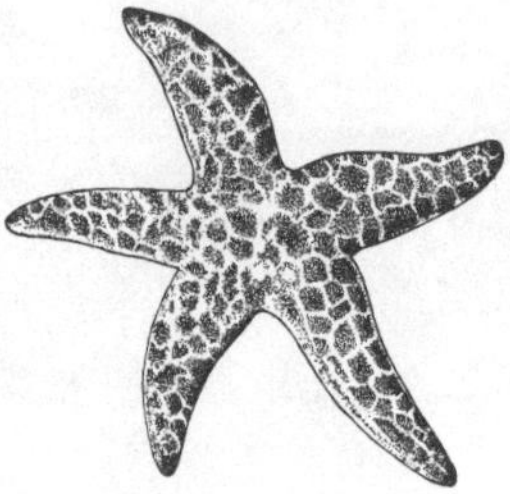

Starfish

Characteristics: Stars symbolize hope, and if the starfish is your totem you maintain a hopeful attitude even during difficult times. Your optimism and openness let you spot opportunities everywhere, and to make the best of them. Even if you fail at something, you can renew yourself and regain what you've lost: you learn from your experiences and grow stronger. You move through life in a slow, steady manner and keep your feet on the ground; you don't need to make a big splash. By following your "star" and remaining true to your own vision, you can succeed.

Strengths: Optimism, vision, rejuvenation, beauty, persistence

Weaknesses: Defensiveness

How to use this creature's power: What's your fondest wish? Ask a starfish to help you make it come true. When you feel all is lost and you're about to give up, call upon a starfish to restore your hope and help you rejuvenate yourself. A starfish can point the way to becoming a star in your own right.

Symbolic meanings: When a starfish appears, it may tell you to look for your star and let it guide you. Stars signify good fortune, so your luck could be about to improve. You might see a starfish in waking life or a dream when your "star" qualities are about to emerge.

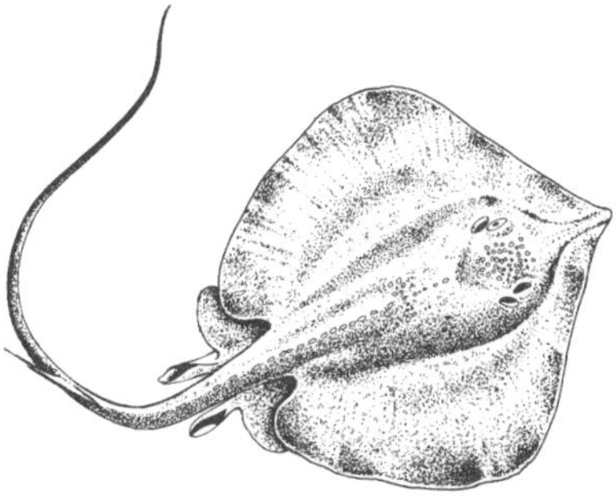

Stingray

Characteristics: You're a master at riding the currents and adapting to shifting circumstances. Often you go along to get along. You move through life with ease and flexibility, maneuvering deftly around problems. Your sensual grace and natural rhythm could make you a wonderful dancer. Emotionally sensitive, you react strongly to other people's words and behavior. When you feel threatened, you lash out sharply to defend yourself, and your sting can be deadly. Most of the time, though, you prefer to avoid conflict and don't feel a need to attract attention or make waves.

Strengths: Flexibility, grace, rhythm, intuition

Weaknesses: Tendency to overreact, defensiveness, vindictiveness

How to use this fish's power: A stingray can teach you how to "read" other people and test the waters in a situation, before taking action. It can also show you how to navigate smoothly through emotional ups and downs. When you need to strike, a stingray can help you hit your target with deadly accuracy.

Symbolic meanings: If you encounter a stingray in real life or a dream, it might be a warning to defend yourself, or it could advise you to examine a situation carefully before lashing out hurtfully. Are you being vindictive? If so, a stingray's appearance may tell you to be more understanding and accepting.

Swordfish

Characteristics: Your dynamic personality and dashing presence command attention wherever you go. Strong, confident, and independent, you chart your own course in life and don't let anyone or anything get in your way. You know what you want and feel completely entitled to grab it, and you usually succeed at whatever you undertake. Forthright and intelligent, you wield your verbal skills like a mighty sword and cut down others with your sharp wit. Some people may consider you cutthroat or arrogant, but you aren't deterred by the opinions of others; you enjoy making waves and thrive on controversy.

Strengths: Physical power, self-confidence, independence, ambition, intelligence

Weaknesses: Ruthlessness, tactlessness, bullying behavior, arrogance

How to use this fish's power: When you want to blow your opponents out of the water, ally yourself with a swordfish. A swordfish can teach you how to slice through obstacles and get what you want. If you feel timid or weak, ask a swordfish to show you how to be strong and bold, and to overcome your fears.

Symbolic meanings: If you see a swordfish in the waking world or a dream, it may advise you to be more adventurous and independent. Take what you want without hesitation. Be direct. In some cases, a swordfish's appearance might warn you that you're about to be verbally attacked by someone or that someone close to you is not interested in your well-being.

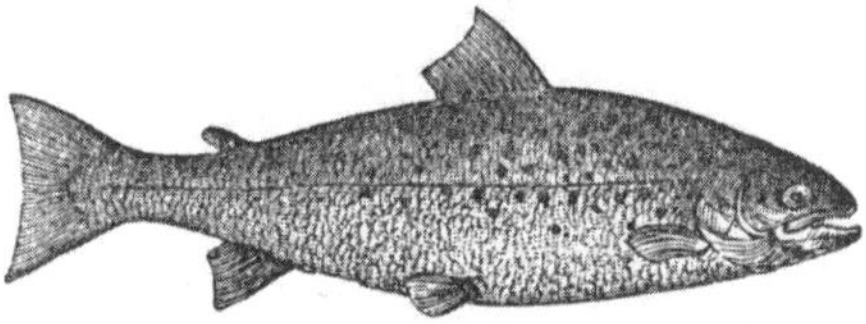

Trout

Characteristics: Your strong convictions and sense of purpose enable you to face challenges with courage and determination and to swim bravely onward even when you're going against the current. Independent and forthright, you believe in yourself and the validity of your ideas. Your colorful personality and intelligence attract people who are inspired by your vision. Consequently, you could rise to a position of leadership in a company, organization, or movement. It's important for you to get input from others, however, in order to remain objective and balanced.

Strengths: Independence, intelligence, self-worth, vision, honesty, vivaciousness, courage

Weaknesses: Arrogance, narrow-mindedness, rebelliousness, stubbornness, cunning

How to use this fish's power: When you want to express your opinions but fear reprisal or rebuke, ask a trout to lend you its self-confidence. A trout can also help you stay focused on your objectives, even when swimming against the tides.

Symbolic meanings: If you see a trout, it may recommend following your own truth regardless of what other people think. Believe in yourself and the importance of your mission in life. In the midst of an emotional situation, a trout may tell you to "come up for air" in order to see things more clearly.

Tuna

Characteristics: With your strength and speed, you could excel in athletics and other activities that require physical power. Water sports in particular might interest you. You know how to use your energy to best advantage, and to conserve it when necessary. Sociable and team-minded, you function best in groups, and your circle of associates may include various types of people. However, you have a passionate nature and can be a bit of a hothead at times, and learning to manage your feelings might be one of your challenges. It's important for you to eat a healthy diet; avoid foods with lots of additives and pesticides.

Strengths: Athletic ability, physical power, sociability

Weaknesses: Quick temper, sensitivity to toxins

How to use this fish's power: Ask a tuna to help you excel in any type of athletic activity, especially water sports. A tuna can also teach you how to use your skills and energy effectively, and to work cooperatively with other people, especially people whose backgrounds, talents, or experiences are different from yours.

Symbolic meanings: If you encounter a tuna in the real world or a dream, it could warn you to be alert to potential danger. You can find safety in numbers. A tuna's appearance might also advise you to eliminate toxins in your diet, as well as toxic people or emotions that could harm your health.

INDEX

Air element, 18–19
Albatrosses, 124
Alligators/crocodiles, 208
Alpacas, 48. *See also* Llamas
Andrews, Ted, 40, 46
Animal medicine, 37–39
Animals, 47–121. *See also* Birds; Fish and sea creatures; Insects; Reptiles and amphibians
alpacas, 48
anteaters, 49
antelopes, 50
armadillos, 51
badgers, 52
bats, 53
bears (black/brown), 54
beavers, 55
black panthers, 56
boars, wild, 57
bobcats, 58
buffalo/bison, 59
bulls, 60
camels, 61
cats, 62
cheetahs, 63
chimpanzees, 64
chipmunks, 65
cougars/mountain lions, 66
cows, 67
coyotes, 68
deer, 69
dogs, 70
dolphins, 71
donkeys, 72
elephants, 73
elk, 74
ferrets, 75
foxes, 76
giraffes, 77
goats, 78
gophers, 79
gorillas, 80
griffins, 81
groundhogs, 82–83
horses, 84
hyenas, 85
jaguars, 86
kangaroos, 87
koalas, 88
lions, 89
llamas, 90
manatees/dugongs, 91
mice, 96
minks, 92
moles, 93
monkeys, 94
moose, 95
opossums, 97
otters, 98
oxen, 99
pandas, 100
pigs, 101
polar bears, 102
porcupines, 103
rabbits, 104
raccoons, 105
rams, 27, 106
rats, 107
reindeer, 108
rhinoceroses, 109
seals, 110
sheep, 111

skunks, 112
snow leopards, 113
squirrels, 114
tigers, 115
unicorns, 116
walruses, 117
weasels, 118
whales, 119
wolves, 120
zebras, 121
Animal-Speak (Andrews), 40, 46
Anteaters, 49
Antelopes, 50
Ants, 186
Anubis, 17
Armadillos, 51
Aztecs, 17

Badgers, 52
Bats, 53
Bears, black/brown, 54
Bears, polar, 102
Beavers, 55
Bees, 187
Beetles, 188
Birds, 123–83
albatrosses, 124
blackbirds, 125
bluebirds, 126
blue jays, 127
canaries, 128
cardinals, 129
chickadees, 130
chickens, 131
cockatoos, 132
condors, 133
cormorants, 134
cranes, 135
crows/ravens, 136
cuckoos, 137
doves, 138
ducks, 139
eagles, 140
falcons, 141
finches, 142
flamingos, 143
geese, domesticated, 144
geese, snow (blue), 173
grackles, 145
grouse, 146
gulls, 147
hawks, 148
herons, 149
hummingbirds, 150
kingfishers, 151
loons, 152
magpies, 153
meadowlarks, 154
mockingbirds, 155
orioles, 156
ostriches, 157
owls, 158
painted buntings, 159
parrots, 160
peacocks, 161
pelicans, 162
penguins, 163
Pheasants, 164
phoenixes, 165
pigeons, 39, 166
puffins, 167
quail, 168
roadrunners, 169
robins, 170

roosters, 171
sandpipers, 172
snow (blue) goose, 173
sparrows, 174
starlings, 175
storks, 176
swallows, 177
swans, 178
turkeys, 179
vultures, 180
waxwings, 181
woodpeckers, 182
wrens, 183
Bison/buffalo, 59
Black, symbolism of, 29
Black bears, 54
Blackbirds, 125
Black panthers, 56
Blue, symbolism of, 29
Bluebirds, 126
Bluefish, 228
Blue jays, 127
Boars, wild, 57
Bobcats, 58
Book overview, 9–10
Brown, symbolism of, 29
Brown bears, 54
Buddhism, 18
Buffalo/bison, 59
Bulls, 60. *See also* Cows
Buntings, painted, 159
Butterflies, 189

Camels, 61
Canaries, 128
Cardinals, 129
Carp, 229. *See also* Koi/goldfish
Catfish, 230
Cats, 62
black panthers, 56
bobcats, 58
cheetahs, 63
cougars/mountain lions, 66
jaguars, 86
lions, 89
snow leopards, 113
tigers, 115
Celtic beliefs, 15
Centipedes, 190
Chameleons, 209
Charms, making, 43–44
Cheetahs, 63
Chickadees, 130
Chickens, 131. *See also* Roosters
Chimpanzees, 64
Chipmunks, 65
Clams, 231
Cobra, 39, 221
Cockatoos, 132
Cockroaches, 191
Colors, meanings of, 29
Communicating with spirit animals, 30–31
Conches, 233
Condors, 133
Coral, 232
Cormorants, 134
Cougars/mountain lions, 66
Cows, 67. *See also* Bulls
Coyotes, 17, 68. *See also* Wolves
Crabs, 234
Cranes, 135

Crayfish, 235
Crocodiles/alligators, 208
Crows/ravens, 136
Cuckoos, 137
Cycles, seasonal and diurnal, 20–21

Damselflies/dragonflies, 192
Deer, 69. *See also* Antelopes; Elk; Moose; Reindeer
Dinosaurs, 210
Diurnal cycles, 20–21
Dogs, 70
Dolphins, 71
Donkeys, 72
Doves, 138. *See also* Pigeons
Dragonflies/damselflies, 192
Dragons, 211
Dragons, Komodo, 217
Dreams, spirit animals in, 28–29. *See also specific animals*
Ducks, 139
Dugongs/manatees, 91

Eagles, 140
Earth element, 18–19
Earthworms, 212
Eels, 236
Egypt, Joseph and, 28
Egyptian deities, 16–17, 20, 67
Elemental connections, 18–19
Elephants, 73
Elk, 74
European beliefs, 15–16

Falcons, 141
Familiars, 38–39
Ferrets, 75
Fetishes, making, 43–44
Finches, 142
Fire element, 18–19
Fireflies/lightning bugs, 193
Fish and sea creatures, 227–58. *See also* Reptiles and amphibians
  bluefish, 228
  carp, 229. *See also* goldfish/koi
  catfish, 230
  clams, 231
  conches, 233
  coral, 232
  crabs, 234
  crayfish, 235
  eels, 236
  flounder/sole, 237
  flying fish, 238
  goldfish/koi, 239
  jellyfish, 240
  leeches, 241
  lobsters, 242
  manatees/dugongs, 91
  octopi, 243
  oysters, 244
  salmon, 245
  sand dollars, 246
  sea anemones, 247
  sea horses, 248
  sea urchins, 249
  sharks, 250
  shrimp/prawn, 251
  snails, 252
  squid, 253
  starfish, 254
  stingrays, 255
  swordfish, 256

trout, 257
tuna, 258
whales, 119
Flamingos, 143
Fleas, 194
Flies, 195. *See also* Dragonflies/damselflies; Fireflies/lightning bugs
Flounder/sole, 237
Flying fish, 238
Foxes, 18, 76
Frogs, 213

Ganesh, 17
Geckos, 214
Geese, domesticated, 144
Geese, snow (blue), 173
Gila monsters, 215
Giraffes, 77
Goats, 78
Gods and goddesses, worldwide, 16–18, 67
Gold, symbolism of, 29
Goldfish/koi, 239
Gophers, 79
Gorillas, 80
Grackles, 145
Grasshoppers, 196
Gratitude, expressing, 36–37
Green, symbolism of, 29
Griffins, 81
Groundhogs, 82–83
Grouse, 146
Gulls, 147
Hawks, 148
Healing, animal medicine and, 37–39
Herons, 149
Honoring totem animals, 36–37
Hopler, Whitney, 122
Hornets/wasps, 205
Horses, 84
Horus, 17
Hugin (thought), 17–18
Hummingbirds, 150
Hyenas, 85

Iguanas, 216
Inari, 18
Indigo, symbolism of, 29
Insects, 185–205
ants, 186
bees, 187
beetles, 188
butterflies, 189
centipedes, 190
cockroaches, 191
dragonflies/damselflies, 192
fireflies/lightning bugs, 193
fleas, 194
flies, 195
grasshoppers, 196
ladybugs, 197
locusts, 198
mosquitoes, 199
praying mantises, 200
scorpions, 201
spiders, 202
termites, 203
ticks, 204
wasps/hornets, 205

Jaguars, 86
Jellyfish, 240
Jesus, 18
Journeying, shamanic, 40–43

Kangaroos, 87
Kingfishers, 151
Koalas, 88
Koi/goldfish, 239
Komodo dragons/monitor lizards, 217

Ladybugs, 197
Leeches, 241
Leopards, snow, 113
Lightning bugs/fireflies, 193
Lions, 89
Lizards, worm, 225
Llamas, 90. *See also* Alpacas
Lobsters, 242
Locusts, 198
Loons, 152

Magpies, 153
Manatees/dugongs, 91
Mascots, animals as, 16
Meadowlarks, 154
Medicine, animal, 37–39
Meeting spirit animals, 25–26
Mice, 96
Minks, 92
Mockingbirds, 155
Moles, 93
Monitor lizards/Komodo dragons, 217
Monkeys, 94
Montesquieu-Avantès, France, 13
Moose, 95
Mosquitoes, 199
Mountain lions/cougars, 66
Mouse, 96
Munin (memory), 17–18
Myths
- alligators/crocodiles in, 208
- animal deities and, 18
- black panthers in, 56
- composite creatures, 20
- conches in, 233
- coyotes in, 68
- dinosaurs in, 210
- griffins in, 81
- peacocks in, 161
- phoenixes in, 165
- seals in, 110
- sea turtles in, 219
- shapeshifting, 40
- snakes in, 220
- toads in, 223

Octopi, 243
Odin (Woden), 17–18
Opossums, 97
Orange, symbolism of, 29
Orioles, 156
Ostriches, 157
Otters, 98
Owls, 158
Oxen, 99
Oysters, 244

Painted buntings, 159
Paleolithic peoples, 13
Pandas, 100
Panthers, black, 56

Parrots, 160
Peacocks, 161
Pelicans, 162
Penguins, 163
Pets
  familiars and, 38–39
  as totem animals, 24
Pheasants, 164
Phoenixes, 165
Pigeons, 39, 166. *See also* Doves
Pigs, 101. *See also* Boars, wild
Pink, symbolism of, 29
Polar bears, 102
Porcupines, 103
Prawn/shrimp, 251
Praying mantises, 200
Predators and prey, 32–33
Puffins, 167
Purple, symbolism of, 29

Quail, 168
Quetzalcoatl, 17

Rabbits, 104
Raccoons, 105
Rainbow Serpent, 17
Rams, 27, 106. *See also* Sheep
Rats, 107
Ravens/crows, 136
Recognizing spirit animals, 26–28
Red, symbolism of, 29
Reindeer, 108
Reptiles and amphibians, 207–25
  alligators/crocodiles, 208
  chameleons, 209
  dinosaurs, 210
  dragons, 211
  earthworms, 212
  frogs, 213
  geckos, 214
  Gila monsters, 215
  iguanas, 216
  Komodo dragons/monitor lizards, 217
  salamanders, 218
  sea turtles, 219
  snakes (nonpoisonous), 220
  snakes (poisonous), 221–22
  toads, 223
  tortoises, 224
  worm lizards, 225
Rhinoceroses, 109
Rhythms, of animals, 20–21
Roadrunners, 169
Robins, 170
Roderick, Timothy, 8
Roosters, 171. *See also* Chickens
Ryujin, 17

Salamanders, 218
Salmon, 245
Sand dollars, 246
Sandpipers, 172
Scarabs (beetles), 188
Scorpions, 201
Sea anemones, 247
Sea horses, 248
Seals, 110
Seasonal cycles, 20–21
Sea turtles, 219
Sea urchins, 249
Sekmet, 17

"Shadow side," of you, 32–33
Shamanic journeying, 40–43
Shamans, 41
Shapeshifting, 40, 41
Sharks, 250
Sheep, 111. *See also* Rams
Shrimp/prawn, 251
Silver, symbolism of, 29
Skunks, 112
Snails, 252
Snakes (nonpoisonous), 220
Snakes (poisonous), 221–22
Snow (blue) goose, 173
Snow leopards, 113
Sole/flounder, 237
Sparrows, 174
Sphinx, 20
Spiders, 202
Spirit animals. *See also specific animals*
  acting like, 39–40
  actions/disposition of, 31
  communicating with, 30–31
  in dreams, 28–29
  elemental connections, 18–19
  familiars and, 38–39
  habitat and behavior of, 30
  historical perspectives, 13–14, 15–16
  knowing yours, 23–24
  meeting, 25–26
  one or many, 14–16
  pets as, 24
  predators, prey and, 32–33
  primary, 15, 25–26. *See also* Totem animals
  recognizing, 26–28
  seasonal/diurnal cycles and, 20–21
  symbiotic relationships between, 32–33
  terminology associated with, 31
  traits of, 30
  worldwide animals, 16–18
Spirit animals, working with, 35–44
  about: overview of, 35–36
  acting like animal, 39–40
  animal medicine and, 37–39
  honoring your totem animal, 36–37
  making charms and fetishes, 43–44
  shamanic journeying and, 40–43
  shapeshifting and, 40, 41
  vision quests and, 43
Squid, 253
Squirrels, 114
Standley, Dr. Loretta, 37–38
Starfish, 254
Starlings, 175
Stingrays, 255
Storks, 176
Subconscious, 32–33
Swallows, 177
Swans, 178
Swordfish, 256
Symbiotic relationships, between animals, 32–33
Symbolism
  of animal's actions, 31
  of animal's habitat and behavior, 30
  of animal's traits, 30
  of colors, 29

communicating with animals and, 30–31
of dreams, 28–29

Team mascots, 16
Terminology, animal, 31
Termites, 203
Ticks, 204
Tigers, 115
Toads, 223
Tortoises, 224. *See also* Turtles, sea
Totem animals. *See also* Spirit animals
creature(s) associated with, 32–33
defined, 14
familiars and, 38–39
honoring, 36–37
one or many, 14–16
pets as, 24
sharing with others, 37
tips for meeting, 26
working with. *See* Spirit animals, working with
your personal, 14–16
zodiac animals as, 16
Trout, 257
Tuna, 258
Turkeys, 179
Turtles, sea, 219. *See also* Tortoises

Unicorns, 116

Venefica, Avia, 184, 206, 226
Vision quests, 43
Vultures, 180

Walruses, 117
Wasps/hornets, 205
Water element, 18–19
Waxwings, 181
Weasels, 118
Whales, 119
White, symbolism of, 29
White Buffalo Calf Woman, 17
Wild boars, 57
Wolves, 120
Woodpeckers, 182
Worldwide animal deities, 16–18
Worm lizards, 225
Worms, earthworms, 212
Wrens, 183
www.angels.about.com, 122
www.whats-your-sign.com, 184, 206, 226

Yellow, symbolism of, 29
Yoga poses, 39

Zebras, 121
Zodiac animals
bulls, 60
Chinese, 18, 101
crabs, 234
pigs, 101
rams, 27, 106
as totems, 16
Western, 18, 27

About the Author

Skye Alexander is the author of more than thirty fiction and nonfiction books, many of them about metaphysical and healing topics. Her stories have been published in numerous anthologies internationally, and she's also written for magazines, newspapers, radio, and TV. She divides her time between Texas and Massachusetts.